T0208912

Counsellors' Skills in Existentialism and Spirituality

Counsellors—Do they Possess the Skills and the Insights to Hold This Sacred Space?

Mary Gilligan Cuddy

BALBOA.
PRESS

A DIVISION OF HAY HOUSE

Balboa Press books may be ordered through booksellers or by contacting:

Balboa Press
A Division of Hay House
1663 Liberty Drive
Bloomington, IN 47403
www.balboapress.com
1 (877) 407-4847

Print information available on the last page.

ISBN: 978-1-9822-0358-0 (sc)
ISBN: 978-1-9822-0361-0 (e)

Balboa Press rev. date: 05/19/2018

CONTENTS

Summary vii

Abstract...ix

Acknowledgements..xi

List of Appendices...xiii

Introduction..xv

Chapter 1   Existentialism-Philosophical Underpinnings.................1

Introduction...1

1.1 The Existential Movement: European and
American Moorings 1

1.2 The Existential Phenomenological Paradigm...........7

1.3 Significant Thinkers in Existentialism: Jean-
Paul Sartre and Irvin Yalom 12

1.4 Essence of Existentialism: A Philosophy of
Meaning...17

1.4.1 Isolation and Meaning..................................17

1.4.2 Freedom and Individuality 18

1.4.3 Authenticity and Responsibility....................22

1.5 Fundamental Divisions within Existential
Philosophy: Atheistic, Jewish and Christian
Existentialism..24

Summary 31

Chapter 2   Victor Frankl's Logotherapy-Healing Through
             Meaning 32

             Introduction 32

             2.1 Biographical Sketch: Victor Frankl 32

             2.2 A Philosophy of Meaning: The Nature of
                 Existence and the Meaning of Life 38

             2.3 On the Meaning of Love 46

             2.4 Death, Meaning and Self-Transcendence 49

             2.5 Logotherapy in Practice 55

             Summary 58

Chapter 3   Spirituality: Its Essential Essence in the Work of
             Anthony de Mello 60

             Introduction 60

             3.1 Anthony De Mello: His Life and Times 61

             3.2 De Mello's Spirituality: Its Essential Essence 67

             3.3 Happiness, Pain and Suffering 71

             3.4 Attachment, Detachment and Discernment 73

             3.5 Liberty 75

             3.6 A Spirituality within the Christian
                 Existentialist Tradition 78

             Summary 82

Conclusion 85
Bibliography 95

             Journals 98

             Encyclopedia Articles 98

             Online Sources 98

             Unpublished Material 99

Appendix A 101

SUMMARY

This study examines an existential approach to therapy, one which appears to reflect and move in synchronicity with life's flow, rendering it a highly valid and effective response to the existential anguish which has engulfed the mindset of the twenty-first century. The writer endeavours to explore a number of key existential themes such as death, freedom, isolation and meaning. Existentialism presents possibilities and a freedom to 'be', emanating out of personal responsibility for one's life choices. The movement has evolved over the decades and countless theologians, philosophers and psychologists have built upon the deposits of knowledge and life experience of our ancestors.

Frankl presents a three-dimensional view of man's existence to incorporate the somatic, mental and spiritual dimensions in arriving at what the writer deems a highly effective existential approach, that of logotherapy. Existential frustration, prevalent in society, arises out of man's striving to find concrete meaning in life, which can lead to neurosis. Noogenic neurosis stems from illness 'out of spirit' as opposed to 'in the spirit'. Logotherapy aims to educate the individual towards responsibility for one's life and encourages a 'free to' psychology, an alternative approach to that of Frankl's comrades in the field of psychotherapy. Frankl links freedom with responsibility. It is up to each individual to decide 'from what' he is driven or motivated and 'to whom' he is responsible. Frankl sums up these two facets of the human condition through a simple admonition from Maria von Ebner-Eschenback "Be the master of your will and the servant of your conscience!" (Frankl, 2000a, p.59). Conscience acts as a prompter, indicating the direction we should go in a given situation. It is this enduring spiritual freedom, available to all, which ultimately gives life its very meaning and purpose. Though we cannot predict the future we can decide our attitude and respond as persons of inner strength and resilience. The author suggests that such a perspective, though it may not change personal circumstances or the problems we face, does, however, increase our ability and effectiveness in dealing with the problems which life throws our way.

Anthony de Mello, a Jesuit priest, successfully sought out and combined what was good and true in spiritual practices from Eastern culture in an attempt to complement Christian and Western approaches. Religion, as De Mello envisaged, is geographical, influenced and conditioned by the culture from which it emerges. Spirituality, as shown by the research, is universal, it embraces all people to include Christian, non-Christian and doubters alike. His intercultural approach had a major impact, helping people from all backgrounds to find God in all things. De Mello suggests that lack of awareness and reality in our modern world is a cancer. The writer concurs with De Mello's assertion that until man becomes self-aware, he or she has no right to interfere with anyone else or with the world. The purpose of this research was to explore the theme of spirituality set within an existential framework and to examine the role of the counsellor in dealing with existential and spiritual concerns within this sacred space. The writer suggests that counsellors have a duty of care to explore spiritual and existential issues with the patient. Existential counsellors must explore in depth their own spirituality in order to fully understand the true nature of man. The writer values the existential emphasis on freedom and responsibility and the person's capacity to redesign his or her life by choosing with awareness. The effective counsellor can only lead or direct a client towards his or her spiritual core, leaving the ultimate decision with the individual whether to accept or reject this spiritual dimension. The writer suggests that it is the presence of Spirit within the spiritual encounter which heals, transforming and integrating man into wholeness. The author urges the counsellor to humbly embrace this opportunity to explore and encounter the spiritual dimension within the therapeutic relationship as a core counselling objective.

ABSTRACT

This study examines an existential approach to therapy, one which appears to reflect and move in synchronicity with life's flow, rendering it a highly valid and effective response to the existential anguish which has engulfed the mindset of the twenty-first century. The writer explores a number of key existential themes such as death, freedom, isolation and meaning. Existentialism presents possibilities and a freedom to 'be', emanating out of personal responsibility for one's life choices. Victor Frankl was a central figure in the development of existential therapy. He presents a three-dimensional view of man's existence to incorporate the somatic, the mental and the spiritual dimension, arriving at what the writer deems a highly effective existential approach, that of logotherapy. Existential frustration, prevalent in society, arises out of man's striving to find concrete meaning in life, which can lead to neurosis. Noogenic neurosis stems from illness 'out of spirit' as opposed to 'in the spirit'. Logotherapy aims to educate the individual towards responsibility for one's life and encourages a 'free to' psychology, an alternative approach to that of Frankl's comrades in the field of psychotherapy. Frankl links freedom with responsibility, it is up to each individual to decide 'from what' he is driven and 'to whom' he is responsible. Though we cannot predict the future we can decide our attitude and respond as persons of inner strength and resilience. Anthony de Mello, a Jesuit priest, successfully sought out and combined what was good and true in spiritual practices from Eastern culture in an attempt to complement Christian and Western approaches. Religion, as De Mello envisaged, is geographical, influenced and conditioned by the culture from which it emerges. Spirituality is universal, it embraces all people to include Christian, non-Christian and doubters alike. His intercultural approach had a major impact, helping people from all backgrounds to find God in all things. De Mello suggests that lack of awareness and reality in our modern world is a cancer. The writer concurs with De Mello's assertion that until man becomes self-aware, he or she has no right to interfere with anyone else or with the world.

The purpose of this research was to explore the theme of spirituality set within an existential framework and to examine the role of the counsellor, in dealing with existential and spiritual concerns, within this sacred space. The author concludes that counsellors have a duty of care to the patient and must explore in depth his or her own spirituality in order to fully understand the true nature of man. Finding a meaningful life is about finding the right attitude and becoming absorbed in that process. The author values the existential emphasis on freedom and responsibility and the person's capacity to redesign his or her life by choosing with awareness. The effective counsellor can only lead or direct man towards his or her spiritual core, leaving the ultimate decision with the individual whether or not to accept or reject his or her spiritual dimension. The writer suggests that it is the presence of Spirit within the spiritual encounter which heals, transforms and integrates man into wholeness. The author urges the counsellor to humbly embrace this opportunity to explore and encounter the spiritual dimension within the therapeutic relationship as a core counselling objective.

ACKNOWLEDGEMENTS

I dedicate this book to my beloved parents
Martin and Catherine Gilligan
(R.I.P. 2010, 2018)

LIST OF APPENDICES

Appendix A: Frankl's Three Dimensional Model of Man from which are projected Max Scheler's concentric layer model together with the strata model

INTRODUCTION

The search for spiritual truth and the deeper meaning in life is a cornerstone of every culture. In these early first years of the twenty-first century, we find ourselves living in a profoundly pluralistic world of diverse cultures and traditions (O'Rourke, TCD Lecture Notes, 2010). Pain and tragedy beset human beings in many ways throughout their lives. The boundaries of human freedom are set by a universal order, which expresses itself in an absolute manner. Birth and death are the most obvious of these boundaries (Van Deurzen, 2002, p.10). It is necessary to think about death if we are to think significantly about life. The transient nature of life, coupled with our inevitable earthly demise, equate to giving life its very meaning. If we affirm life and live in the present as fully as possible, we will not be obsessed with life's ending. Existential counselling is a voyage into self-discovery both for client and therapist, a journey that delves deeply into the world as perceived and experienced by the client (Corey, 2001, p.156).

The spiritual dimension goes to the heart of therapy and confronts the therapist with an understanding both of himself and his client, which has profound implications for the therapeutic undertaking. The primary aim of this research is to explore the role of the counsellor within the context of spirituality and the 'givens' of human existence, with a view to uncovering whether or not the counsellor possesses the skills and insights to hold this sacred space. Throughout this study the writer has focused primarily on the role of the counsellor. However, she is of the opinion that the same principles which apply to the counselling profession apply to all who work within a pastoral care profession. As a dedicated primary teacher, the author wishes to educate herself, in a personal attempt to gain mastery over the art of living by clarifying, reflecting upon and understanding life, so that life's challenges can be welcomed and enjoyed instead of feared and avoided. The words of Kahlil Gibran resonate deeply with her in terms of what it means to be effective within a teaching, counselling or pastoral care profession:

> No man can reveal to you aught but that which already lies half asleep in the dawning of your knowledge. The teacher who walks in the shadow of the temple, among his followers, gives not of his wisdom but rather of his faith and his lovingness. If he is indeed wise he does not bid you enter the house of his wisdom, but rather leads you to the threshold of your own mind (Gibran, 1926, p.76).

It is the writer's contention that education is clearly broader than subject knowledge, in that it involves a loving response in order to meet the needs of the whole child, emotionally, socially, physically and spiritually. It entails accompanying each individual child along an inner journey in which he or she is accepted, respected and understood, leading ultimately to independent responsibility. The key to growth is freedom and as a teacher one can educate the individual towards responsibility. By encouraging self-awareness, reflection and freedom of expression from an early age, the author suggests that teachers can challenge pupils into conscious awareness of their existence. In doing so the child is brought face to face with his or her spiritual dimension, confronted with the responsibility to accept or reject that aspect of being.

Chapter One provides an overview of existentialism as the writer's theoretical orientation of choice. The writer suggests that within its elusive framework lies the possible response to the mystical yearnings of many twenty-first century men and women and has within it the seeds of reconciliation between man and his or her spiritual self, between cultures, and between the world's greatest faiths. Chapter Two explores the work of Victor Frankl, a leading existential thinker. He is chosen as a major theorist and philosopher through whom to ground this body of research and through whom the theme of spirituality can be explored within the context of counselling. Frankl brought religion into counselling in a very subtle way without placing emphasis or superiority on any one religious orientation. Such an intercultural approach is inclusive of all people of varying religious and non-religious orientations, allowing one to resonate deeply with his philosophy. Chapter Three explores the theme of spirituality with a view to addressing the similarities and differences, if any, between the commonly misused terms, spirituality and religion. Anthony de Mello, a highly influential figure of recent times, revealed creatively the presence of God in new and sometimes surprising ways. He successfully sought out and combined what was good and true in Western, Eastern and Christian tradition. De Mello's patchwork approach may be considered a strength or a weakness; however, it represents a universal spirituality which is inclusive and respectful of all people. With the focus on self-awareness and presence of God in all things De Mello illuminates the transitory nature of life which, he suggests, flows like a river.

The existential approach to counselling allows for flexibility in dealing with individual clients as it focuses on values, attitudes and a shared philosophy rather than techniques and particular therapeutic strategies. Clients deserve the deepest respect for what he or she is, regardless of how inadequate or worthless he or she may feel. An existential practitioner must make understanding life his or her priority, exploring the essential issues and questions that life raises. It is considered essential for people to have a consistent framework of reference within which to reflect on their lives and organise their experience. As van Deurzen states, "Unless the practitioner is experienced and creative enough to meld different approaches and assumptions into a new and consistent synthesis, the result may be extremely confusing" (van Deurzen, 2002, p.2). The writer endeavours in this study to highlight the personal responsibility that man has in the first instance, to uncover his or her true existential nature, and, secondly, when acting as a professional counsellor to explore key existential concerns with the client.

ONE

Existentialism-Philosophical Underpinnings

Introduction

Chapter one traces the origins of existentialism as a whole, drawing out the salient points in terms of its essential essence. Existentialism emerged in various pockets of Europe following the Second World War and made its way to America through philosophers and psychologists such as Rollo May, James Bugental and Irvin Yalom. Existentialism is a philosophy about the concrete individual, to which it attributes 'freedom' its supreme value and 'authenticity' its primary virtue in an attempt to defend the intrinsic value of the 'free organic individual'. It seeks to revive philosophy as a way of life, by delving into the core of one's being and drawing out the truth of one's existence, giving rise to authenticity.

1.1 The Existential Movement: European and American Moorings

The word 'existence' – *Exsistenz* in German – derives from the Latin *'ex'* meaning 'out' as in 'exit' (goes out) and the verb *'sistere'* (to stand), from which we can deduce that existence means 'to stand out' (Patterson & Watkins, 1996, p.430). Existentialism emerged spontaneously during the revolutionary age of the 1940s and 1950s in France and Germany, as one of those movements of revolt against over-systematisation in philosophy. Existentialism reached its high point as a phenomenon of Western culture following the end of the Second World War. *Exsistenz* suggested the future, that which has yet to occur, as being rich in possibilities and presented a flicker of hope in the face of new realities for many Westerners. In France, the existential movement achieved popular success and was seen as "the child of liberation" (Flynn, 2006, p.104). Its origins can be traced back over the centuries to the Hellenistic period and to the Ancient Greeks, a time when the philosopher was regarded as a kind of 'doctor of the soul'. Aristotle, Socrates, Descartes, St. Augustine, Blaise Pascal and German Romantics of the 19th century encouraged an understanding of philosophy as care of the self.

Existentialism does not represent a single movement or school of thought and rejects the notion that it is a philosophy; yet it is commonly acknowledged as a philosophy regarding the concrete individual. It seeks to revive philosophy as a way of life; its main thread anchored in subjective truth – a moral rather than scientific truth by which the authentic person lives, leading primarily to a way of life – a lived experience. Soren Kierkegaard, one of the first existentialist philosophers, conveys this notion when he states, "the thing is to understand myself, to see what God really wishes *me* to do; the thing is to find a truth which is true for *me*, to find *the idea for which I can live and die*" (Kierkegaard, 1846, cited in Solomon, 1974, p.9). Karl Jaspers, another key existentialist philosopher further suggests existence as a forward motion in which we must "apprehend truth from our own source" based on the historical traditions of our time; we can ask primal questions, however, our position is never at the beginning but rather in relation to the beginning, which is in part determined by the current historical tradition (Jaspers, 1935 cited in Kaufmann, 1956, p. 160). We must not dismiss the contribution of past generations in what has been handed down to us but rather build on this knowledge by seeking a thorough understanding of such historical sources and how they impinge upon us at our source, together with the examination of subsequent thoughts which are aroused within the depths of our being, giving us ownership of original thought. Jaspers reminds us:

> The content of truth depends upon our appropriating the historical foundation. Our own power of generation lies in the rebirth of what has been handed down to us. If we do not wish to slip back, nothing must be forgotten; but if philosophizing is to be genuine our thoughts must arise from our own source (Jaspers, 1935 cited in Kaufmann, 1956, p.160).

During and following World War II, Western culture saw a gradual demise of religious faith and devotion as it submerged beneath a wave of contemporary art and scientific discovery during the Renaissance and scientific revolution. "Because of the impact of Christianity on the Western World the revival of the ancient schools of thought at the beginning of the modern period was not only a revival but also a transformation" (Tillich, 2000, p.18). The Renaissance started a movement which was looking at the future creatively, seeking the new in it. Existentialist thought permeated European intellectual life at this time, carving its imprint in the literature, education, art and psychology of the era (O'Rourke, Lecture Notes TCD, 2009a). Kierkegaard claims that the source of all misfortune, particularly within the religious and political spheres is disobedience, an unwillingness to obey: "it is not doubt of religious truth but insubordination against religious authority which is the fault of our misfortune and the cause of it" (Kierkegaard, cited in Kaufmann 1956, p.106). Western culture had lost its way and realised that the bedrock upon which to build and move forward was absent; the keystone of which can be traced back to Christianity: "Christianity, against a background of belief in original sin, that we first find this wallowing in man's deprivation and this uncompromising concentration on the dark side of man's inner life" (Kaufmann, 1956, p.13).

Existentialism focused on understanding deep human experiences in an attempt to resolve man's dilemma, the fragmentation of contemporary life, such as meaninglessness, alienation and isolation. Existential philosophy, much to its peril and acclaim, drew from a major orientation in philosophy, to arrive at a person-centred, individualistic psychology, a psychology of freedom which is often associated with a certain kind of humanistic philosophy (Corey, 2001). The hallmark of existentialist thought is the role of the 'free, responsible individual' captured eloquently by Polonius, who famously uttered in Shakespeare's Hamlet, "to thine own self be true". Rollo May, a key philosopher responsible for the development of existentialism defined it thus:

> The endeavour to understand man by cutting below the cleavage between subject and object which has bedevilled Western thought and science and shortly after the Renaissance...It arose specifically just over a hundred years ago in Kierkegaard's violent protest against the reigning rationalism of his day, Hegel's 'totalitarianism of reason', to use Maritian's phrase (May et al., 1958, p.11).

To avoid persecution during World War II many Westerners fled to America, bringing with them a wealth of literature, art, culture and psychology. Rollo May is generally credited as the first major figure responsible for bringing existentialism from Europe to the United States. May, born in Ada, Ohio, grew up in Michigan and moved to Europe from 1930 until 1933, during which time he indulged in his artistic pursuits and for a while studied with Alfred Adler, founder of individual psychology. Following a period of self-exploration into the meaning of his life, May's trip culminated in a nervous breakdown, forcing him to review and challenge old values in an attempt to replace them with new ones. This marked the beginning of his journey into existential psychology. In 1934 he returned to America and began to study basic questions related to human existence at the Union Theological Seminary, where he became deeply influenced by the theologian and existential philosopher, Paul Tillich, a refugee from Germany (Hergenhahn & Olsen, 2007). May's philosophy was empowering, hopeful and optimistic – if one has the courage to 'be' and accept responsibility for their life, they can 'choose' the type of person they wish to become. May recognized the courage required to establish values to enhance personal growth, an all too often painful process. A book entitled *Existence: A New Dimension in Psychiatry and Psychology* (1958) was central to the introduction of existential therapy to America (Corey, 2001).

Other significant thinkers such as James Bugental, Irvin Yalom and Victor Frankl have also been credited with making a significant impact upon American existentialism (Corey, 2001). At the heart of Bugental's life-changing approach is the client's subjective world into which the client and therapist aim to delve in an attempt to examine, review and revise one's answers to life's existential questions, emerging with new "answers to begin living authentically" (Bugental, cited in Corey, 2001, p.144). Frankl's contribution, which will be examined in more detail in Chapter Two, brought religion into psychology in a very subtle way. He was regarded as a 'depth psychologist' yet referred to himself as a 'height psychologist'. Having spent time as a prisoner in the Nazi concentration camps of Auschwitz and Dachau, Frankl was in a position to implement and personally experience the truths expressed by existential philosophers and writers. He spoke of self-transcendence and finding the supra-meaning in life – the former in relation to one's unique ability to extend beyond the realm of self or possibility and the latter in connection with one's belief in a God and the afterlife (O'Rourke, TCD Lecture Notes, November 2009a). Frankl placed love as the highest value to which man could aspire, and claimed that meaning and purpose in life could be found through our actions and deeds, by experiencing a value such as love, or through suffering. Man can be robbed of all that he humanly possesses with the exception of one core attribute – the freedom to choose: "to choose one's attitude in any given set of circumstances, to choose one's own way" (Frankl, 1963 cited in Corey, 2001, p.141). Frankl gained a lived life experience of existential psychology and has shown how man can triumph in the face of adversity by choosing to 'be'.

As a cultural phenomenon of the twenty-first century, existentialism has had its day, though a residue of its existence can still be traced within subcultures. Its demise came about in the second half of the twentieth century, the student rebellion of 1968, which proclaimed, "all power to the imagination", which captured the spontaneity, and utopian hope, and possibly, the ultimate futility of that student uprising, epitomised the notion that as beings in-situation we are creatures of possibility (Flynn, 2006, p.104). Existentialism was eclipsed by two successive schools of thought, namely structuralism and post-structuralism. The former sought out impersonal and necessary structures of cultural practice in an objective and scientific manner while the latter's anti-humanism served to "decentre the subject", leaving the responsible individual as a mere "place holder" within the impersonal structure of which they are usually ignorant (Flynn, 2006, p.116). The pull of modern society is towards conformity and away from individualism. According to Jasper, a prominent German existentialist, "the sclerosis of objectivity is the annihilation of existence" (Jasper, 1935 cited in Methuen 1996, p.10). Modern man has immersed himself in materialism, technologism, consumerism and the mass media of communication, all of which give rise to an air of indifference, now prevalent among individuals towards their fellow man:

> Twentieth-century man has lost a meaningful world and a self which lives in meanings out of a spiritual center. The man-created world of objects has drawn into itself him who created it and who now loses his subjectivity in it. He has sacrificed himself to his own production (Tillich, 2000, p.139).

The twenty-first century man has traded his individuality in an attempt to fit in with the 'masses', wherein members are mostly trained as opposed to being educated (Solomon, 1974). Where the authentic individual struggles against the 'masses', individuality is no longer a starting point, it's an achievement (Flynn, 2006). Kierkegaard reminds us: "The crowd in fact is composed of individuals; it must therefore be in every man's power to become what he is, an individual. From becoming an individual no one, no one at all, is excluded, except he who excludes himself by becoming a crowd" (Kierkegaard, 1859 cited in Kaufmann, 1956, p.99). Values and attitudes, the very fabric of human interaction and relations, which once served to provide meaning and purpose, have now been eroded, leaving a human shell void of intrinsic meaning and sense of personal worth. Man has become separate, and believes himself to be separate, from his source. Modern man has become a slave to ambition and has traded his 'free organic nature' for an existence in which the external world is the source of all he possesses. He has become de-spiritualized, relentless in his search for instant gratification, to accumulate, get ahead and fit into his growing social network; he has failed to stop and simply 'be'; he has failed to seek the hidden treasure within his spiritual core; he has failed to seek God. In the face of growing political, economic, social and environmental uncertainty, modern man, as aptly cited by Jaspers, remains "free to open his life – but in anguish – to the influence of a living God, or in pride to deny and repel Him" (Jaspers, cited in Methuen 1996, p.10).

1.2 The Existential Phenomenological Paradigm

European philosophy of the 1960s and 1970s was viewed as a more pessimistic approach as it encouraged a philosophical investigation of human *being*, whereas the American humanistic psychology of the same era "emphasized human potential, the core goodness of human beings and their innate ability to grow and even self-actualize" (Woolfe et al., 2010, p.131). Although obvious overlaps exist between humanistic and existential philosophy there are fundamental differences between the two. Humanists 'are' from the time of their birth in possession of both positive and negative aspects of human nature which are brought to the fore by motivational and environmental factors conducive to self-actualization. Existentialists 'become' as they explore and develop their potential and should accept responsibility for the choices they make to create meaning in life. Both groups, however, embrace concepts such as "freedom, choice, values, personal responsibility, autonomy, purpose, and meaning", encouraging the therapist to enter the subjective world of the client (Corey, 2001, p.171). The metaphor of the acorn and the oak tree is used effectively to capture the underlying vision of the humanistic movement: if conditions are favourable the acorn or positive aspects of the person grow and mature naturally "towards its actualization as an oak" (Corey, 2001, p.173). Existentialists find meaning from outside of themselves; they view this path towards self-actualization as an endless series of choices in life based on external factors as opposed to an internal bank of resources from which they can draw meaning.

Existentialists take the person's consciousness as the subject matter, analyzing awareness of all types: "Phenomenology is the study of that which is given in human consciousness" and as humans are conscious beings, consciousness is studied as an intact, meaningful phenomenon (Hergenhahn & Olsen, 2007, p.506). 'What it means to be a human being', a key consideration from which emerged the existential-phenomenological tradition, takes into account man's subjective experience, personal meaning and self-worth (Woolfe et al., 2010). Existential phenomenological psychology is a combination of two philosophical traditions, phenomenology and existentialism. Human existence is categorised into three 'existence spheres' or stages in which one must live simultaneously, and can be traced back to the existential philosophical tradition, to thinkers such as Dostoyevsky, Kierkegaard and Sartre. According to Kierkegaard, human existence is based on the following stages: the aesthetic relates to that of immediate requirement; the ethical, which is a transitional sphere, relates to the past as repentance and the future as obligation; while the religious sphere is concerned with personal fulfilment.

> There are three existence-spheres: the aesthetic, the ethical, the religious. The metaphysical is abstraction, there is no man who exists metaphysically. The metaphysical, ontology, is but does not *exist*; for when it exists it is in the aesthetic, in the ethical, in the religious, and when it is the abstraction of or the *prius* for the aesthetic, the ethical, the religious. The ethical sphere is only a transitional sphere, and hence its highest expression is repentance as a negative action. The aesthetic sphere is that of immediacy, the ethical

is that of requirement… the religious sphere is that of fulfilment, but note, not such a fulfilment as when one fills a cane or a bag with gold, for repentance has made infinite room, and hence the religious contradiction: at the same time to lie upon seventy thousand fathoms of water and yet be joyful (Kierkegaard, 1940, p.430).

According to Kierkegaard most people live within the aesthetical sphere of existence, incapable of choosing to become a 'self' indifferent to the past and to the future, where rules of right and wrong do not apply (Flynn, 2006). Individuals within this sphere ultimately become fragmented. They lose or fail to uncover the unique, unifying power of the personality, the holiest, most sacred part, their hidden treasure. When you lose that inner, most holy part of the self, according to Kierkegaard, "[In your present state] you are incapable of love because love means self-giving and you have no self to give" (Kierkegaard, cited in Flynn, 2006, p.36). The one who cannot love is the unhappiest one of all.

Concepts important to existential phenomenological psychology include the German word *Daesin* to express an essential quality of human life and *Welt* meaning world, and in this context the structure of meaning and meaningful relationships in which a person exists. *Mitwelt* is literally the 'with-world' in terms of interpersonal relationships, being with others. *Umwelt* translates literally as 'around-world' the physical aspects of the internal and external environment to include the body. *Eginwelt* or 'one's own world' relates to a person's consciousness or relationship to one's self. Emmy van Deurzen, a leading existentialist therapist, refers to a fourth dimension, *Uberwelt,* which points to the abstract and metaphysical aspects of living, the world of "experience where people create meaning for themselves and make sense of things" (2002, p.87). Within this realm man formulates his ideals, values, beliefs and principles by which to live, giving rise to his overall world view. These divisions represent four widely accepted categories of living within existential psychology. Man can live simultaneously in all four dimensions, each of which must be considered in unison to fully account for individual existence.

Daesin (*Da* 'there', *sein* 'to be') literally translates as 'to be there'. Heidegger highlights the essence of existential counselling and psychotherapy when he suggests that "we are ourselves the entities to be analysed" (Heidegger, cited in Solomon, 1974, p.96). Dasein is the study of a person as a being-in-the-world: "The term indicates that the focus of interest for the existentialist is a particular person experiencing and interpreting the world at a particular time in a particular place" (Hergenhahn & Olsen, 2007, p.506). According to Heidegger, the world of Daesin is a "with-world" such that Dasein, every day employs "Being-with-one-another" (Heidegger, cited in Solomon, 1974, p.101). Human existence is complex – constantly moving and changing. We are faced with the task of choosing, accepting, rejecting, reviewing and altering who we are, in order to 'be':

> That way of being which characterizes human being from the outset is something which it *is* in so very immediate a way that it can only be rendered *susceptible to analysis* at the outcome of a long and laborious detour which eventually brings thinking back to its original point of departure (Macann, 1993, p.204).

Phenomenology, pioneered by Edmund Husserl and Heidegger, is mainly concerned with the subjective experience of the individual, getting back to the 'experience' itself, maintaining a 'here and now' focus in relation to that experience:

> Ultimately the existential counsellor wishes to explore concertedly with the client all of life, not simply the random issues that emerge in session, whose transient importance may only fade into the background of the larger scheme of life that went unexplored (Corey, 2001, p.160).

Key insights can be attained through the unfolding of that experience; it is the manner in which the experienced is perceived that in turn shapes one's reality of events and in the broader sense their world view:

> Most existential therapists agree that a crucial part of therapy involves tuning into the client's world by attending closely not only to what is said, but also to the way in which it is said and, beyond this, to the client's demeanour as a whole (Woolfe et al., 2010, p.135).

Our mental acts are unique in that they extend beyond themselves towards another, giving rise to the most significant and widely accepted claim of phenomenology, the principle of intentionality. According to Heidegger, "we must keep in mind that the expression 'phenomenon' signifies that which shows itself in itself, the manifest" (1962, p.51). Our mental acts form a bridge between ideas in the mind and the external world. Consciousness is therefore a way of being in the world as every mental act 'intends' an object already in the world. The point of phenomenological method is not in the 'explaining' of a cause but in the 'seeing' or grasping of the presence of a thing (Flynn, 2006). Jaspers considers, "man cannot be comprehended on the basis of himself, and as we confront man's being, there is disclosed the other through which he exists" (Jaspers, cited in Kaufmann, 1956, p.179). Sartre was of the view that 'being' has appearance, meaning, nature, essence only for individual man, or only as man gives it such. He declares, "The being of an existent entity is precisely what it appears...Our theory of the phenomenon has replaced the reality of the thing, by the objectivity of the phenomenon" (Sartre, cited in Cochrane, 1956, p.69).

The existential philosophical tradition can be traced to Dostoyevsky, Kierkegaard and Sartre. Existentialists are of the view that humans are future-orientated and concerned with the meaning of life: "in this view people are in the ongoing process of becoming" (Monte & Sollod, 2003, p.424). Existentialists are concerned with man as a form of Being and seek to explore the relationship between one's Being, and one's Being in relation to the world. Van Deurven suggests that "exploring clients' relationships to the structure of their natural world is a crucial step in the full understanding of their way of being in the world" (2002, p.63). If, according to Sartre, existence precedes essence, one is not born an individual; the direction one takes in life ultimately leads to an existential 'choice'. There is no 'objectively' correct path to choose, one makes it the right path by one's follow through (Methuen, 1948).

Being human involves change, engaging in a process of constantly becoming. Without a permanent or fixed essence, the potential and possibility for change can of itself evoke much anxiety (Woolfe et al., 2010). According to existential philosophers, "existential anxiety or *Angst* is that basic unease or malaise which people experience as soon as they are aware of themselves. It is the sensation that accompanies self-consciousness and awareness of one's vulnerability when confronted with the possibility of one's death" (Van Deurzen, 2002, p.34).

A lot of energy is bound up in seeking and maintaining a stable sense of self, resisting change and the possibility of change. Man must reflect upon aspects of living and accept responsibility for engaging with life whilst endeavouring to understand and interpret the meaning which he himself attributes to those same life experiences (Woolfe et al., 2010).

1.3 Significant Thinkers in Existentialism: Jean-Paul Sartre and Irvin Yalom

Born in Paris in 1905, Jean-Paul Sartre was one of the most renowned and influential philosophers of the 20th century. Following his graduation from *École Normale Supérieve* in 1928, Sartre became a teacher and devoted himself to literary work. In 1939 he joined the army and spent nine months as a prisoner of war in Germany. Following his release in 1941 he joined the resistance movement, where he remained until 1944 (Cochrane, 1956). Though he never married, he remained throughout his adult life with Simone de Beauvoir, one of the most famous women of her age. Sartre achieved great success as a literary figure. Noted as a distinguished writer, he contributed generously to the fine arts plays, novels and philosophical works and was offered (though he declined) the Nobel Prize for literature in 1964. Sartre claimed, "there is only committed knowledge", which led to his use of the phrase "committed literature", believing that one must take responsibility for the written word (Sartre, cited in Flynn, 1997, p.94). In our present time of social oppression and economic exploitation he calls for active opposition; the key to its alleviation is literature. "It is to freedom, and to freedom alone", Sartre affirms, "that the writer is committed" (Sartre, cited in Guerlac, 1997, p.94). Sartre, himself an atheist, postulated in an essay entitled 'Cartesian Freedom' that in the absence of a belief in God, the entire 'world' is our creation for which we hold total responsibility; we are without excuse. Our very existence is a brute fact, we are and we need not be. By actively choosing we can, and remain free to, invent; we are responsible either way, to opt for or against freedom itself (Sartre, cited in Methuen, 1948): "No rule of general morality can show you what you ought to do; no signs are vouchsafe in this world" (Sartre, cited in Kaufmann, 1956, p.356). The interpretation of these signs rest within the individual, regardless of what, or to which higher source, one aspires; our moral values are a result of our creative 'choices'. Sartre is of the view that:

> Man makes himself; he is not found ready-made; he makes himself by the choice of his morality, and he cannot but choose a morality, such is the pressure of circumstances upon him (Sartre, cited in Methuen 1948, p.59).

Sartre suggests that "man is nothing else but what he purposes, he exists only in so far as he realises himself, he is therefore nothing else but the sum of his actions, nothing else but what his life is" (Sartre, 1996, p.47). In existential psychology one's entire life is an ongoing series of choices. Failure to choose is also a choice; becoming an individual is a task to be undertaken and sustained. According to Sartre, "the first effect of existentialism is that it puts every man in possession of himself as he is, and places the entire responsibility for his existence squarely upon his shoulders" (Sartre, 1996, p.31).

Central to Sartrean existentialism is the notion that 'existence precedes essence' –man is what he makes of himself. "Man first of all exists, encounters himself, surges up in the world – and defines himself afterwards" (Sartre, 1996, p.30). One must begin from the subjective. In choosing essence, one's first choice should be one of 'freedom', not an individual freedom but rather a collective freedom which seeks the liberation of all. This notion became the basis for his argument, in his famous public lecture delivered shortly after the end of the war in 1945, *Is existentialism a Humanism?*

> Obviously, freedom as the definition of man does not
> depend on others, but as soon as there is commitment, I
> am obliged to will the liberty of others at the same time
> as mine. I cannot make liberty my aim unless I make
> that of others equally my aim (Sartre, cited in Methuen
> 1948, p.62).

At the very heart of and central to existentialism is the humanistic motto, you can always make something out of what you've been made into, "by which everyman realises himself in realising a type of humanity" (Sartre, cited in Methuen, 1948, p.55). Whatever the situation the possibility exists to extend beyond the circumstances due to the existential assumption that one can always transcend their facticity, the givens of a situation such as, race and nationality, talent and limitations. Transcendence is always toward something, and dialectic, according to Sartre, presupposes a certain "action of the future as such" (Flynn, 1997, p.144). Sartre claims that from an existential point of view, man is not the end since he is still being determined, concluding his lecture with the declaration that existentialism as a movement is not atheistic. He declares,

> Rather, that even if God existed that would make no
> difference from its point of view. Not that we believe

> God exists, but we think that the real problem is not
> that of his existence; what man needs is to find himself
> again and to understand that nothing can save him
> from himself, not even valid proof of the existence of
> God (Sartre, cited in Methuen, 1948, p.68).

"A core existential conflict is the tension between the awareness
of the inevitability of death and the wish to continue to be" (Yalom,
1998b, p.172). Irvin Yalom was born in the ghettos to a Jewish family
in Washington D.C. in 1931. Yalom described his relationship with his
mother as fractured and, though he knew her to be intelligent, found
her "vain, controlling, intrusive, suspicious, spiteful, highly opinionated
and abysmally ignorant" (Yalom, 1999. p.3). His interest in writing and
psychology has led to the successful publication of both non-fiction and
fictional literature. Yalom narrows the lens of his existential focus to
highlight four ultimate concerns or 'givens' of existence: death, meaning
in life, isolation and freedom:

> I have found that four givens are particularly relevant to
> psychotherapy: the inevitability of death for each of us
> and for those we love; the freedom to make our lives as
> we will; our ultimate aloneness; and, finally, the absence
> of any obvious meaning or sense to life. However grim
> these givens may seem, they contain the seeds of wisdom
> and redemption (Yalom, 1998b, p.345).

"Though the physicality of death destroys us, the idea of death may
save us (Yalom 2002, p.126). Yalom approaches the subject of death
in a calm, matter-of-fact way, in an attempt to elicit the patient's prior
experience of death and expose symptoms of death anxiety, claiming
such an approach is often very reassuring to the patient (2002, p.128).
He takes his lead from the many great philosophers who have concluded
that "to live well is to learn to die well" (Yalom, 2002, p.125). Yalom's
answer to the crucial question of meaning in life can be discovered in a
number of areas. These include a deeply held religious belief, altruism,

self-transcendence, dedication to a cause, creativity, self-actualization, developing a self identity and growing into an independent, autonomous adult ready to pursue life's meaning as a mature adult (O'Rourke, Lecture Notes TCD, 2010). "Freedom means that one is responsible for one's choices, actions, one's own life situation" (Yalom, 1989, p.8). Our actions, choices and failures to act, shape who we become as individuals: "we ultimately design ourselves. We cannot avoid this responsibility, this freedom" (Yalom, 2002, p.137). Yalom refers to existential isolation as an "unbridgeable gap between self and others, a gap that exists even in the presence of deeply gratifying relationships", and distinguishes it from interpersonal and intrapersonal isolation (Yalom, 1989, p.10). Isolation in general, for the most part, is concealed from us; however, it comes to the fore as death approaches and we are faced with what may be considered the loneliest of human experiences.

> If we do not come to terms with existential isolation, we tend to search for solace in our interpersonal relationships. Rather than relate authentically, with caring, we use the other for a function (Yalom, 1998b, p.271).

Our reality is based upon our perception of the world and "is processed through our neurological and psychological apparatus" (Yalom, 2002, p.138). In its existential sense 'freedom' refers to the absence of external structure, leaving full responsibility with the individual, as the author of his or her own world or life design (Yalom, 1998a). Beneath us it is groundless, nothingness, with despair emanating from our shared experience of existences. Yalom's inner personal focus is based on the assumption that people fall into despair due to an inability to maintain gratifying relationships. He postulates that the group dynamic in counselling offers the perfect arena to identify and modify the pathology of individual members. Similar to Bugental, Yalom views the role of the psychologist as one of 'fellow traveller' and emphasizes that a significant amount of interaction takes place in the "here-and-now" relationship (Yalom, 1989, p.8). Yalom defines existential psychotherapy as a dynamic approach to therapy which focuses on concerns that are rooted in the individual's experience (2002, xvi). Arthur Schopenhauer suggests, "death-anxiety is least where self-realization is most" in Yalom's novel *The Schopenhaur Cure*, claiming that those who have lived an unfulfilled life experience it to a greater degree (Yalom, 2005, p.340). As meaning-seeking creatures thrown into a universe that has no meaning we must endeavour to create a meaning robust enough to bear one's life (Yalom, 1998a). Based upon his therapeutic experiences Yalom has come to the assumption that "basic anxiety emerges from a person's endeavours, conscious and unconscious, to cope with the harsh facts of life, the 'givens' of existence" (Yalom, 1998b, p.345).

1.4 Essence of Existentialism: A Philosophy of Meaning

1.4.1 Isolation and Meaning

We must accept and face the reality that we as human beings are ultimately alone. We must be able to stand alone and accept the reality that we cannot "depend on anyone else for our own confirmation; that is, we alone must give a sense of meaning to life, and we alone must decide how we will live" (Corey, 2001, p.149). We must endeavour to establish an honest authentic relationship with ourselves, in the hope that we can derive strength from the realisation that though we are separate we are also uniquely individual. Existential isolation, as defined by Yalom (1998a), refers to isolation from creatures and from the world. It should not be confused with loneliness associated with interpersonal isolation or isolation from parts of oneself, as in intrapersonal isolation. We must accept the reality that as individuals we enter the world alone and must leave it alone. No matter how close we come in terms of relationships to significant others there remains an 'unbridgeable gap'. We strive to be part of something, to reach out beyond ourselves and become part of the greater whole and therein lies the tensions between our need to feel apart and our awareness that we are ultimately alone

(Yalom, 1998a). Logotherapy, which will be explored in detail in Chapter Two, is designed to help clients find meaning in life: "It holds that human suffering (the tragic and the negative aspects of life) can be turned into human achievement by the stand an individual takes in the face of it" (Corey, 2001, p.151). Van Deurzen, in her book *Existential Counselling and Psychotherapy,* offers a concrete framework and practical methods to enable people find meaning in life, through reflection and self-awareness. Existentialism is a way of broadening one's perspective, and unlike more traditional approaches – psychoanalysis and behaviourism – it does not set out to change people or problem solve. Van Deurzen draws an analogy between art and living, suggesting that perfection is a result of error and practice. She considers, "The aim of existential therapy and counselling is to gain mastery over the art of living, so that life's challenges can be welcomed and enjoyed instead of feared and avoided" (Van Deurzen, 2002, p.19).

Existential therapy provides the basis from which people can draw out, develop and put into practice their own unique talents and create a pattern of living to reflect these new realities. As with the training of any new skill, the therapeutic relationship provides the framework within which committed clients can monitor the consistency of these new skills and thought patterns within their everyday life. "New meanings and possibilities are revealed and with them the source of personal motivation and courage" (Van Deurzen, 2002, p.23). Once the client commits to reviewing old thought patterns and takes responsibility for their life, they become increasingly open to the new possibilities. Existential therapy can provide the encouragement and support required by the client to orientate themselves, "by the compass" of their own conscience (Van Deurzen, 2002, p.51).

1.4.2 Freedom and Individuality

Existentialism has long been referred to as an 'individualistic' philosophy. Becoming an individual in our society is an achievement, a task to be undertaken and sustained, as opposed to a starting point. Existing as an individual may involve a certain degree of risk taking and is always dynamic, a continuously evolving state of renewal, emerging and becoming; it is never static and complete. The pull of modern society is from individualism, towards conformity, to act as 'they' do. Kierkegaard described this movement as a process of levelling, giving rise to a reflective and passionless age. In order to activate this process and reduce all things to the same level, it is first necessary to create its spirit, a phantom, and that phantom is, according to Kierkegaard, 'the public' or 'the plebs', whilst Nietzsche speaks of the 'herd', Heidegger of 'Das Man' and Sartre the 'one' (Kaufmann, 1956).

> A public is everything and nothing, the most dangerous
> of all powers and the most insignificant: one can speak
> to a whole nation in the name of the public and still the
> public will be less than a real man, however unimportant"
> (Kierkegaard, cited in Solomon, 1974, p.7).

Kierkegaard attributes the rapid development of 'a public' to that of the popular press, which in itself is an abstraction. The press has become a highly influential means of fuelling the notion of 'a public' by mediating the thought process of individuals with some higher level thinking associated with the 'masses'. The press as an expression of the abstract, the impersonal, is, according to Kierkegaard, "a fundamental source of modern demoralization" (Kierkegaard, cited in Soloman, 1974, p.88). Nietzsche considers in *Thus Spoke Zarathustra,* "No shepherd and one herd! Everybody wants the same, everybody is the same: who ever feels different goes voluntarily into a madhouse" (Nietzsche, cited in Solomon, 1974, p.51). It appears all too easy to conform, to fit in with the 'masses' rather than to stand out as a individual and, as Heidegger so aptly puts it, "everyone is the other, and no one is himself" (Solomon, 1974, p.103). If man is deluded into believing that one's life is controlled and influenced by others, it is only logical that one will become preoccupied with trying to change or reform 'them' in order to affect a change in one's own world. Kierkegaard encourages man to turn back and seek what it means to be a 'single individual', seek true freedom by availing of that which has been given to every man, "freedom of thought" (Kierkegaard, cited in Soloman, 1974, p.8). Instead man demands freedom of speech as compensation.

Man has the freedom of thought, therefore, he has the freedom to choose, the outcome of which is reflected by the manner in which one chooses to live. In the words of Sartre, "we are our choices" (Corey, 2001, p.147). Freedom exists only as potential and can be increased by expanding consciousness (Hergenhahn & Olsen, 2007, p.507). Sartre declares that freedom can have no other aim but itself and once man realizes that values depend solely upon himself, "he can will only one thing, and that is freedom as the foundation of all values" (Sartre, 1996, p.61). According to Van Deurzen, human freedom exists within boundaries set by a universal order, the two most obvious being birth and death, together with basic physical and biological principles (Van Deurzen, 2002). Each individual has the freedom to choose and decide upon the meaning of their life, and the value and meaning of those experiences are a result of one's attitude and choices. Yalom (2002) suggests that freedom runs deeper than our individual life design. On the basis of Kant's philosophy we must take responsibility for the form and meaning of our internal world together with that of our external world: "We play a central role in constituting that world – and we constitute it as though it appears to have an independent existence" (Yalom, 2002, p.138).

Philosophers such as Heidegger and Kierkegaard argue that the ultimate freedom of man lies in the fact that he is more than his facticity, by opting to live out of a spiritual centre, which is grounded in the presence of the Divine at the core of his Being. Kierkegaard so eloquently conveys this notion when he states:

> In relation to their system most systemizers are like a man who builds an enormous castle and lives in a shack close by; they do not live in their own enormous systematic buildings. But spiritually that is a decisive objection. Spiritually speaking a man's thought must be the building in which he lives – otherwise everything is topsy-turvy" (Solomon, 1974, p.8).

According to Heidegger, "the glory of 'man' is his openness to Being" (Flynn, 2006, p.52). Man's glory lies in his openness and attentiveness to the 'call' of the 'holy' or divine dimension in his daily life giving rise to profound and endless possibilities. Kierkegaard maintains that man can reach God or an awareness of God, through an inward relationship of oneself to oneself and to the subjectivity of others based on the truth – truth as subjectivity. Objective truth or knowledge is more removed from the truth: "Kierkegaard asserted the proposition, as you believe so you are: Faith is Being" (Soloman, 1974, p.192). This inwardness culminates in passion within the person, and in his writings explores, as previously mentioned, the three spheres of existence. The aesthetic life of pleasure, the ethical life of moral principal and duty, and the 'leap of faith' into the religious sphere of fulfilment are studied by Kierkegaard to resolve the problems posed by passion.

> To him who follows the narrow way of faith no one can
> give him counsel, him no one can understand. Faith is
> a miracle, and yet no man is excluded from it; for that
> in which all human life is unified is passion, and faith
> is a passion (Kierkegaard, cited in Solomon, 1974, p.17).

Kierkegaard's preferred mode of existence is to make "a 'leap' to the religious, that is, the Christian way of life" (Kierkegaard, cited in Solomon, 1974, p.3). He deemed this choice of existence as the highest form of individuation, placing the individual above the universal where goals are of a higher order, namely fidelity to the Divine command. "The thing is to understand myself, to see what God really wishes me to do; the thing is to find a truth which is true for me, to find the idea for which I can live and die" (Kierkegaard, cited in Solomon, 1974, p.9). One can discover the secularized existential path by reflection and must make the choice to take the initial or fundamental 'leap of faith', which gives unity and direction to a person's life. May is of the view that "self-consciousness implies self-transcendence" opening up possibilities for choice, thus the capacity for transcendence is the basis of freedom (Patterson & Watkins, 1996, p.432).

1.4.3 Authenticity and Responsibility

Heidegger has been credited with giving us special use of the term authenticity, *Eigentlich* in German, which translates as 'real', 'own', 'proper', a central existential virtue. The truth which the authentic person lives is primarily a way of life, a manner of existing, or what Kierkegaard referred to as 'subjective truth'. As cited by Sartre, and to a similar degree by Heidegger and Jaspers, "Existentialism must be lived in order to be really sincere. To live as an existentialist means to be ready to pay for this view and not merely to lay it down in books" (Kaufmann, 1956, p.47). One must, like Socrates or Kierkegaard, find a truth worth dying for, and live that truth in all aspects of one's life. Subjective truth focuses on the 'how' as opposed to the 'what' of our beliefs. Truth is more of a moral nature, more a matter of decision than discovery, driven by passion. There is no 'objectively' correct path to choose; one makes it the right choice by one's follow through. To live in-authentically is to live a lie, to deceive oneself is to live in what Sartre deemed 'bad faith'. Sartrean authenticity is grounded in factual truth about the human condition; owning and taking responsibility for the way one intends to live the uncertainties of one's future.

> Before there can be any truth whatever, then, there must be an absolute truth, and there is such a truth which is simple, easily attained and within the reach of everybody; it consists in one's immediate sense of one's self" (Sartre, 1996, p.52).

Like Nietzsche, Sartre remains "faithful to the earth" and says, "Life begins on the other side of despair" (Sartre, cited in Kaufmann, 1956, p.46). As conscious beings we are creatures of possibility, whatever our situation it always includes the possibility of moving beyond it. Our consciousness extends beyond these givens to allow us transcend our facticity. Tillich teaches:

> Man, however, is not just being. He participates
> in nonbeing as well as being...Man alone is able
> to look beyond his own being because he is free to
> transcend every given reality. He has a capacity for self-
> transcendence; "he can envisage nothingness" (Tillich,
> cited in Cochrane, 1956, p.80).

Trying to conform and simply go with the flow, taking on an identity predetermined by others is to live, according to Heidegger, inauthentically as 'they' do; we are denying responsibility for our situation, for our individuation. "This Being-with-one-another dissolves one's own Dasein completely into the kind of Being of 'the Others', in such a way, indeed, that the Others, as distinguishable and explicit, vanish more and more" (Solomon, 1974, p.101). This is the attitude of bad faith to which man becomes enslaved to an image or persona which others have imposed on him and which he has appropriated. Bad faith arises out of the collapse of transcendence, of possibility. Living in bad faith or inauthentically provides an outlet from our responsibility to take control of our lives, a flight from the anguish of our freedom through an attitude of dull resignation to one's fate. According to Sartre, to live inauthentically is to live a lie:

> Since we have defined the situation of man as one of
> free choice, without excuse and without help, any man
> who takes refuge behind the excuse of his passions,
> or by inventing some deterministic doctrine, is a self-
> deceiver" (Sartre, cited in Methuen, 1948, p.60).

A common thread which can be traced to form a delicate yet tangible link between existential philosophisers such as Dostoyevsky, Sartre and Kierkegaard was that of personal responsibility: people have a responsibility for creating the meaning in their lives and for their commitments in various areas of life. From Sartre's perspective, "Man is nothing else but what he makes of himself. Such is the first principle of existentialism" (Sartre, cited in Hergenhahn & Olson, 2007, p.507).

According to Rollo May, "man is the being who can be conscious of, and therefore responsible for, his existence" (May, cited in Patterson & Watkins, 1996, p.431). No one else is responsible for one's condition; not family, heredity, race, culture, caste, environment nor even God can be held accountable. In the words of Sartre, "all that we are, is a result of what we have thought" (Sartre, cited in Solomon, 1974, p.46). Personal freedom and responsibility go hand in hand; they are inseparable. Man is free and it is this very freedom which is the source of much existential anguish. Man is often incapable of choosing to become the 'self', incapable of the risk involved, the commitment, the individuation and abandons his 'either/or' freedom of choice. He remains fragmented, unable to utilise and avail of that freedom which lies within the core of his being, remaining instead in a lowly state of existence whilst the potential to reach beyond the circumstances of his life, to transcend the facticity of his very being lays dormant and untapped. One can choose to do either this or that and there is only a moment when it is indifferent whether he does this or that; not because he has chosen but because he has neglected to choose – because others have chosen for him or because he has become lost to himself. One's entire life is an ongoing choice – failure to choose is also a choice for which we are equally responsible (Corey, 2001).

1.5 Fundamental Divisions within Existential Philosophy: Atheistic, Jewish and Christian Existentialism

"If God did not exist, everything would be permitted" (Dostoevsky, cited in Methuen, 1948, p.37). These words written by Dostoyevsky are, according to Sartre, the starting point for existentialism. Sartre was born into a Christian family, his mother was a Protestant and his father, who died when Sartre was four, was a Roman Catholic (Cochrane, 1956). At the heart of Sartre's atheistic philosophy is his insistence that 'existence precedes essence', our destiny lies in our own hands, we are grounded in ourselves. Sartre suggests:

first of all, man exists, turns up, appears on the scene, and, only afterward defines himself. . . Thus there is no human nature, since there is no God to conceive it. Not only is man what he conceives himself to be, but he is also only what he wills himself to be after this thrust toward existence (Sartre, cited in Cochrane, 1956, p.65).

Existentialism considers that the human being is more than the sum of physical, psychological and social forces. The 'more' is our consciousness by which we can assess and respond to these very forces. The degree of freedom attributed to individuals varies among existentialists according to whether or not they exclude or at least discount belief in God. According to Yalom:

What is important for both Sartre and Camus is that human beings recognize that one must invent one's own meaning (rather than discover God's or nature's meaning) and then commit oneself fully to fulfilling that meaning...Sartre's ethic requires a leap into engagement (Yalom, 1998b, p.280).

Sartre, the only self-declared atheistic existentialist among the major thinkers, held fast to the notion that there is no God and therefore no fixed human nature forcing man to act (Sartre, cited in Encyclopedia Article, 2009). Sartre, like Nietzsche, claims that the level of freedom or autonomy attributed to individuals is absolute, and that man as a creative being should not sacrifice creative choice to a 'higher' value. In the absence of a belief in God, man is free to choose; therefore, he is free to invent himself. As can be seen from his play *Luicifer and the Lord*, Sartre was in a way obsessed with the problem of God, and "more than any other philosopher he has emphasized the extreme need of the absolute without, however, conceding the existence of an Absolute Being as a remedy to this obsession" (Sartre, cited in Cochrane, 1956, p.12). Awareness of one's freedom and subsequent responsibility is the source of much existential anxiety, leading Sartre to conclude that "man is condemned to be free. Condemned, because he did not create himself, yet is nevertheless at liberty, and from the moment that he is thrown into this world, he is responsible for what he does" (Sartre, cited in Methuen, 1948, p.38). Sartre does not believe that his atheistic philosophy is pessimistic, man can take courage and confidence from the fact that one's destiny has yet to be determined and leaves each individual with the responsibility and freedom to give shape to their life and the nature of their being.

> Man cannot will unless he has first understood that he can count on nothing but himself: that he is alone, left alone on earth in his infinite responsibilities, with neither help nor succor, with no other goal but the one he will set for himself, with no destiny but the one he will forge on this earth (Sartre, cited in Cohen-Solal, 2005, p.221).

The source of optimism, therefore, in the face of nothingness, rests exclusive upon the shoulders of man. Man's decisions impact upon humanity as a whole and therefore the freedom and choices of each individual gives shape to the whole of humanity. As such "freedom as the definition of man does not depend on others, but as soon as there is commitment, I am obliged to will the liberty of others at the same time as mine" (Sartre, 1996, p.62). The concept of transcendence in atheistic philosophy is based on the power of some purely inward integrity, an integrity of mastery, a will-to-power, as opposed to obedience to a higher power, namely that of God, as in Christianity (Sartre, 1996).

> Man is all the time outside of himself: it is in projecting and losing himself beyond himself that he makes man to exist; and, on the other-hand, it is by pursuing transcendent aims that he makes himself to exist. Since man is thus self-surpassing, and can grasp objects only

in relation to his self-surpassing, he is himself the heart
and centre of his transcendence (Sartre, 1996, p.67).

Anthony de Mello, a Catholic priest from Bombay, and spiritual
father to hundreds and thousands of people throughout the world,
speaks of a 'universal spirituality', one that is inclusive and healthy
for all people (Ford, 2009). According to De Mello a good Christian
spirituality should be good to all, regardless of culture or religion. De
Mello trained in psychology for the purpose of integrating psychology
and psychological counselling in spirituality and in spiritual guidance.
While working for a master's degree in counselling he became familiar
with transactional analysis and Gestalt psychology and was influenced
by the work of Carl Rogers, Eric Berne, Fitz Perls, and Barry Stevens,
learning from them the art of healing, which he later applied to the
spiritual domain. He did not do so sheepishly, but supplemented all
that he learned with his own methods for effecting change, firstly in
experiencing it himself, then sharing, in the hope of awakening the
experience in others (Nayak, 2007). He states:

> I have wandered freely in mystical traditions that are not
> Christian and not religious and I have been profoundly
> influenced by them. It is to my Church, however, that I
> keep returning, for she is my spiritual home (De Mello,
> 1982, p.xii).

De Mello was of the opinion that direct experience of God was the
natural right of every Christian, not just for the mystic or privileged
few. In 1972, at De Nobili College in Pune, he set up the Institute for
Pastoral Counselling and Spirituality, using his method of counselling
and spirituality which he termed *Sadhana*; a Sanskrit word meaning
"effort towards a goal" (Ford, 2009, p.114). Sadhana incorporates a
number of prayer methods, mental, vocal and petitionary, similar to
that of Ignatius of Loyola. Sadhana was the result of his exposure,
through psychology, to numerous religions and reflected his interest "to
experiment and discern that which was good and true in all spiritualities

27

and traditions" (Nayak, 2007, p.80). De Mello felt there was a need in India to revive the teachings of the old spiritual masters, otherwise spirituality in India would no longer be credible. Sadhana was, in his experience, "a way of looking at reality 'prayerfully' and according to his companions, "Sadhana deals with God, spiritual problems, growth and people in the context of daily life" (Brys & Pulickal, 1995, p.52). His audience was essentially religious people and much of Sadhana was the undoing of strict, rigorous religious formulation. "It is from the oppression of your programming that you need to be liberated. Only then will you experience that inner freedom from which alone all social revolution must arise" (De Mello, 1991, p.18). He sought to help people become whole and healthy by assisting them, first at an existential level, a fundamental step for building a healthy spirituality. By taking an existential approach De Mello shone the spotlight on the art of living spiritually. Sadhana veered away from tradition, structure and routine; by opening one's heart to the guiding spirit one could embrace liberty and real happiness: "Most priests and religious equate prayer with thinking. That is their downfall" (De Mello, 1978, p.7).

"For Father de Mello, spirituality begins to appear where simplicity of life and nature become the natural way of life" (Nayak, 2007, p.50). Contemplation of nature has the potential to take man to mystical heights. He equates the spiritual experience to that of love. It needs to be lived and experienced in order to be fully understood. Through discovery, as opposed to achievement, by self-observation and awareness in the here and now, in the present moment. In one's quest for true happiness or, as he preferred to call it, liberation, there is a need for an attitude of detachment through discernment as "happiness and unhappiness are in the way we meet events, not in the nature of these events themselves" (De Mello, 1989, p.235). Through awareness the heart opens and the conscious state is awakened, allowing one to experience peace, joy, contentment, compassion, love and happiness (Ford, 2009). To receive God's grace the only human effort required on our part is one of watchfulness, to be awake, conscious of God's actions, in order to enable him to act. An extract from De Mello's *One Minute Wisdom* explains it humorously through a story:

'Is there anything I can do to make myself Enlightened?'
'As little as you can do to make the sun rise in the morning.'
'Then of what use are the spiritual exercises you prescribe?'
'To make sure you are not asleep when the sun begins to rise' (1987, p.10).

Yalom reveals fascinating insights with regard to the human condition and man's search for happiness through his written collection of psychological case studies. Through the various fictional characters we get a sense of his religious views and perspective. In his book entitled *Momma and the Meaning of Life*, Yalom reveals his scepticism about the existence of God, believing that the development of religious systems came about in order to "provide comfort and soothe the anxieties of the human condition" (1999, p.23). Though we wish it were so, needing a god and wanting a god, does not make his existence a reality. Yalom reveals

> I can tell you that I very much want to contain the divine spark, I crave to be part of the sacred, to exist everlastingly, to rejoin those I've lost – I wish these things very much but I know these wishes do not alter or constitute reality. I believe that these extraordinary claims require extraordinary evidence – and I mean by that evidence beyond pure experience which as we therapists know is fragile, fallible, rapidly shifting, and vastly influenceable (Yalom, 2002, p.1).

Human beings have an innate need for certainty and have throughout the ages "sought to order the universe by providing explanations, primarily religious or scientific" (Yalom & Leszec, 2005, p.11). Yalom has always been struck by the way in which people who experience a crisis or near-death experience manage to use their experience as an opportunity for change. People are profoundly affected when faced with the reality of their own death and vary in their degree of openness to death, the source of all anxiety. Referring to Spinoza's "being one's own god", Yalom describes how the individual plunges into isolation without the help of the

> myth rescuer or deliverer… we seek relief from the other major alternative denial system: the belief in a personal ultimate rescuer… the belief in a personal god – a figure that might be eternally loving, frightening, fickle, harsh, propitiated, or angered, but a figure that was always there. No early culture has ever believed that humans were alone in an indifferent world" (1998b, p.219).

The best known morality play, *Everyman*, portrays the loneliness of the human encounter with death. The underlying Christian moral revealed to us suggests that "good works within the context of religion provide a buttress against ultimate isolation" (Yalom, 1980, p.357). Religious faith provides the notion of the rescuer or deliverer, in which the journey through life can be lived in the companionship of the ultimate rescuer and need not be taken alone. Religion can provide comfort and help to individuals when faced with unattainable wants in life. It can provide a safe medium through which we heal and dig deep to uncover the roots of anxiety, despair, loneliness and the unfulfilled life. Yalom makes reference to Alfred North Whitehead, who asserts that spiritual belief arises out of isolation: "religion is what the individual does with his own solitariness…and if you are never solitary, you are never religious" (Yalom, 1980, p.398).

Summary

This chapter has shown that existential philosophy is indeed drawn from a wide orientation in philosophy and is justified in its rejection of the notion that it is a single movement or school of thought. The hallmark of the existentialist thought is the role of the 'free, responsible individual', and is often referred to as a person-centred, individualistic psychology associated with a humanistic philosophy. As the research delineates, existentialism considers the human being as more than the sum of physical, psychological and social forces; the 'more' being our consciousness by which we can assess and respond to these very forces. The degree of subsequent freedom attributed to individuals varies among existentialists according to whether or not they exclude or at least discount belief in God. Therein lies the major source of division within existential thought leading to a branching out in terms of religious philosophy and that of secular activism that is still anti-religious. It is the writer's objective to give a balanced overview of both religious and atheistic philosophy in an attempt to shine light upon the central question behind this body of research —whether counsellors possess the skills and the knowledge to hold this sacred space. The chapter therefore culminates with a study of three major existential philosophers, Jean-Paul Sartre, Anthony de Mello and Irvin Yalom. Sartre, a self-declared atheist, rejects the idea that there is any one Truth, only particular truths, and states, "existence precedes essence", leading to the notion that we are grounded in ourselves and ultimately "condemned to be free" (Sartre, cited in Metheun, 1948, p.30, p.38). De Mello, a Catholic priest and spiritual master, teaches a 'universal spirituality' arising out of awareness and self-observation, declaring that "a spirituality that is good, should be good for all" (De Mello, cited in Ford, 2009, p.124. Yalom, a Jewish existentialist, is of the view that religious faith can provide a 'buttress against ultimate isolation' through the notion of a 'myth rescuer or deliverer', offering a safe medium in which individuals can heal and uncover inner truths.

TWO

Victor Frankl's Logotherapy-
Healing Through Meaning

"He who has a *why* to live can bear almost any how" (Nietzsche).

Introduction

This chapter will commence with a biographical sketch of Victor Frankl, an exploration of the personality, influences and life experiences of the man responsible for the creation of existential analytical logotherapy, the 'Third Viennese School of Psychotherapy'. Key concepts of logotherapy will be examined in detail to include the self-transcendent quality of human reality which stems from the spiritual unconscious, within which existential analysis uncovered unconscious religiousness.

2.1 Biographical Sketch: Victor Frankl

Born of Orthodox Jewish parents on March 26, 1905, Victor Emil Frankl grew up in Vienna, home of the renowned psychiatrists Sigmund Freud and Alfred Adler. Frankl had a strong emotional attachment to his parental home and following the death of his father in the Theresienstadt camp, remained with his mother whom he described as a "kindhearted and deeply pious woman" (Frankl, 2000b, p.22). His father was, on the other hand, a just man who possessed a strong sense of duty and remained throughout his life faithful to his principles. Frankl followed suit and referred to himself as a perfectionist, a rational man of the mind yet deeply emotional, a trait which he believed was inherited from his mother. Though religious by nature, Frankl's father was critical in his thinking and may have become the first liberal Jew in Austria. Whilst others were filled with fear when marching to the Theresienstadt camp, his father smiled and told them, "Be of good cheer, for God is near" (Frankl, 2000b, p.25).

Prior to the outbreak of World War II, the environment in which Frankl lived as a child offered a strong sense of emotional safety and security. The family experienced firsthand the effects of poverty, deprivation and the subsequent hardships which arise out of difficult environmental factors beyond one's control. Memories of school days were shrouded in poverty stemming from World War I; begging, stealing and waiting in lengthy queues were common practice. From a tender age Frankl became troubled by the transitory nature of life and death. He did not fear the ephemeral nature of life or the inevitability of death, yet pondered throughout his life on the question of whether the transitory nature of life might destroy its very meaning. This inner struggle led him to the belief that it is death itself which makes life meaningful, a core tenet of logotherapy. Events of the past are preserved in the past, nothing is lost nor can it be altered: "Whatever we have done, or created, whatever we have learned and experienced – all of this we have delivered into the past. There is no one and nothing that can undo it" (Frankl, 2000b, p.29). Frankl developed a passion for reading and became influenced by the work of natural philosophers such as Wilhelm Ostwald and Gustav Theodor Fechner, together with Eduard Hirschmann and Paul Schilder, both of whom were influential students of Sigmund Freud. He became a student of the *Volkshochschule*; these were free schools which had been established for the unemployed and working classes. In 1922, at the age of seventeen, Frankl presented a lecture on *The Meaning of Life* at the people's college in Vienna, from which emerged the seeds of what later became the core tenets of his future theories. He reflects:

Life does not answer our questions about the meaning
of life but rather puts those questions to us, leaving it
for us to find the answers by deciding what we find
meaningful…the ultimate meaning of life is beyond
the grasp of our intellect, but is something we only can
live by, without ever being able to define it cognitively
[internet]. Available at:

http://www.logotherapyinstitute.org/creation.html.
[Accessed 22 November 2010].

His early research and reflections led him to believe that there
was some kind of balancing principle at work in the universe towards
some kind of "'rest state' or equilibrium" (Frankl, 2000b, p.47). He
became fascinated with Freud's *Beyond the Pleasure Principle,* which
paved the way in terms of his interest in psychoanalysis. At the tender
age of sixteen he forged a reciprocal relationship with Freud, initiated
through correspondence. Freud was so impressed with articles by Frankl
that in 1924 he published one such article regarding the "origins of the
mimic movement of affirmation and negation" in the *International
Journal of Psychoanalysis* (Frankl, 2000b, p.49). During this period
Frankl became influenced by the work of Alfred Adler and his theory of
individual psychology. In 1925, Adler included Frankl's scientific paper,
which examined the border area that lies between psychotherapy and
philosophy, in the *International Journal of Individual Psychology.* Frankl
went on to develop concepts which were in opposition to Freud's ideas.
However, he was to hold Freud in high esteem throughout his life and
made a point of "showing him the respect he deserved" (Frankl, 2000b,
p.50). Frankl's humility came to the fore when in a reference to the
influence of Freud he stated, "that a dwarf standing upon the shoulders
of a giant can see farther than the giant himself" (Frankl, 2009, p.23).
During World War II, Frankl found himself within the
concentration camps of Nazi Germany. The horror of war witnessed in
the extermination camps, echoed the private war that each man fought
on a personal level – a fight for self-preservation. Man was confronted

with the truth and reality of his existence, stripped naked in every sense of the word, physically and emotionally to the very core of one's being. Battles were fought and won in the mind and no one proved this better than Victor Frankl. Prisoners entering camp life went through three phases, according to Frankl, the first of which was characterised by initial shock and mental agony at the injustice of one's situation. Frankl soon experienced what he termed the second phase of camp life, apathy, an intensification of the mental agony and the indignation of being treated like an animal, as man was subjected to a sub-human existence leading to a famine of the soul. Apathy was essential, in that it numbed the emotions and feelings, providing a protective and defensive shell into which man could retreat into the solitude of his inner soul (Frankl, 2004, p.40).

Over the course of his internment Frankl embarked on an inward journey which brought him face to face with the truth, that "the salvation of man is through love and in love" (Frankl, 2004, p.49). The exceptionally difficult circumstances presented Frankl with the rare opportunity to grow spiritually beyond himself. By delving into the depths of his inner core, his personality, Frankl sought and utilised the potential therein to ascend beyond himself, reaching great spiritual heights. Frankl found that the consciousness of one's inner value is anchored in higher, more spiritual things, and could not be shaken by camp life. Even in such terrible conditions of psychic and spiritual stress, man can preserve a vestige of spiritual freedom, of independence of mind, "to choose one's attitude in any given set of circumstances, to choose one's own way" (Frankl, 2004, p.74). Man, therefore, was in possession of a spirit, and by acknowledging the presence of that same spirit, it would lead to personal liberation. The spiritual dimension allowed man to transcend his facticity and to emerge from the ashes of despair, to find value and meaning in life. Frankl recalled:

> I sensed my spirit piercing through the enveloping gloom. I felt it transcend that hopeless, meaningless world, and from somewhere I heard a victorious "Yes" in answer to my question of the existence of an ultimate

purpose… '*Et lux in tenebris lucet*' – and the light shineth in the darkness (Frankl, 2004, p.51).

Indeed, Frankl, who had worked on his theory of logotherapy prior to his capture, now had the rare opportunity to explore and test the very nature of the theory which speaks of man's spiritual freedom and responsibility to life. Frankl was aware of man's spiritual dimension and the endless possibilities that lie within his very being. Through a deepening relationship with God, Frankl found freedom, in the form of inner freedom, the kind that cannot be destroyed by the evils of mankind. A vast treasure of riches lie within each and every man, yet only a few make that connection to explore life on a higher spiritual plain which seeks to embrace suffering, believing it to have a greater significance than mere misfortunate, dealt by the hand of fate. Unavoidable suffering is seen as an opportunity to grow and mature as a person, an opportunity to serve a greater good, by taking up one's cross in life and accepting the burden of suffering, just as Christ did for the sake of humanity. Frankl found freedom and momentary solace within the eye of the storm that unfolded around him. He was at peace with his God, remaining faithful to his responsibilities in life, no matter how painful his suffering or the severity of his situation. Despite the limitations imposed upon human freedom within the concentration camps, the good and evil traits of human nature were witnessed on a daily basis. This supports Frankl's theory that man is ultimately free to decide his singularity and uniqueness as an individual, which is beyond the control of external environmental factors. "Everything can be taken from man but one thing: the last of the human freedoms – to choose one's attitude in any given set of circumstances, to choose one's own way" (Frankl, 2004, p.75).

Frankl advanced two serious considerations in terms of self-actualization. We must ask ourselves not only what enables a person in a given profession, but what motivates him or her? Frankl believed his strength as a psychotherapist may have been linked to his talent as a cartoonist. He states:

As a cartoonist, just as a psychiatrist, I can spot the weakness in a person. But as a psychiatrist, or rather a psychotherapist, I can see beyond the actual weaknesses and can also recognize intuitively some possibilities for overcoming those weaknesses. I can see beyond the misery of the situation to the potential for discovering a meaning behind it, and thus to turn an apparently meaningless suffering into a genuine human achievement. I am convinced that, in the final analysis, there is no situation that does not contain within the seed of meaning. To a great extent, this conviction is the basis of logotherapy (Frankl, 2000b, p.53).

When reflecting upon character traits and personality, and how they find expression, Frankl placed significance on pleasures and hobbies, claiming that a hobby can almost develop into a profession. Frankl enjoyed humour and loved telling jokes, so much so that he considered writing a book on the metaphysical background of jokes. He later employed humour as a means of clarifying the difference between treating causes and symptoms. Such was the basis of his explanation to differentiate treating the cause as opposed to the symptoms in relation to sleep disturbance. He tells the story: "during a vacation in the country, a man is awakened early every morning by a crowing rooster. So the vacationer goes to a pharmacy, buys sleeping pills, and mixes them with the rooster's feed. This is the treatment of causes" (Frankl, 2000a, p.40). This colourful sense of humour would later form the basis of one of Frankl's logotherapeutic techniques – paradoxical intention. "One might say as well, that humour helps man rise above his own predicament by allowing him to look at himself in a more detached way (Frankl, 1967, p.16).

Throughout his life, up until his eightieth year, mountain climbing became his most passionate hobby. Frankl enjoyed the solitude of the climb and withdrew to the mountains in order to reflect, gather strength and reach important life decisions, forming what friends considered a link between his passion for mountain climbing and his interest in 'height psychology'. Logotherapy became his height psychology "which takes into account the so-called 'higher aspirations' of the human psyche: not only man's seeking pleasure and power but also his search for meaning (Frankl, 2000a, p.138). He again "reached for the heights" when, at the age of sixty-seven, Frankl completed flying lessons and took his first solo flight in California along the Pacific Coast.

2.2 A Philosophy of Meaning: The Nature of Existence and the Meaning of Life

Frankl has made a significant contribution to the field of existential psychology and philosophy with his theory of *logotherapy*. As a youth Frankl was fascinated by philosophy, psychiatry and psychoanalysis. He professed "logotherapy itself was born in the place of my birth"; however, following his internment during the war, precious manuscripts containing his budding philosophical theories, his life's work, were confiscated and destroyed at Auschwitz. Frankl recalls that moment as the culminating point of the first phase of his psychological reaction: "I struck out my whole former life" (Frankl, 2004, p.27). Frankl was then forced to live out his theories of which he had written within the death camps of Nazi Germany. What he witnessed and experienced far outweighed the written word and what appeared initially as a catastrophic loss was none other than personal gain and insight of the highest degree, sealing his fate as a world renowned author-psychiatrist.

Following the war and his subsequent release from the concentration camps, Frankl entered the third phase of his prison life experience and referred to it as a time of 'depersonalization' or readjustment, during which one faces up to immense personal conflicts. Frankl's enduring motivation and activism towards his life task led him to reconstruct and publish material on logotherapy, from within the study of his apartment in Vienna, which he referred to as "the delivery room" (2000b, p.28). The period spent within the Nazi camps served to confirm his earlier views regarding an existential approach to clinical practice. Logotherapy focuses on the future, on the meaning of human existence and man's search for meaning. Man needs 'something' for the sake of which to live and as early as 1929, Frankl had developed his notion of finding meaning in life and put forward three possibilities. The first of these was creating work or doing a deed; second, by experiencing something or encountering someone; and third, he suggested that through one's own attitude towards unavoidable suffering man can transcend terrible conditions. Man is questioned by life and is answerable through his response to life. Suffering, like death, is an eradicable part of life. If there is meaning to life, it is only natural that there is also meaning in suffering. It is not the meaning in general that matters but rather the specific meaning of a person's life at any given moment. Meaning differs from hour to hour for each individual and it is this fluid, transitory nature of life which gives it its very meaning. We have only one opportunity to realise the potential and possibility, as it presents, in any given moment in time. Frankl repeatedly stated that the only real transitory aspects of life are the potentialities. In the moment they are actualized potentialities are rendered realities which are saved and delivered to the past, where they are irrevocably stored.

Logotherapy, according to Frankl, "keeping in mind the essential transitoriness of human existence, is not pessimistic but rather activistic" (Frankl, 2004, p.124). Man has to take the focus away from him or herself and become active in the pursuit and fulfilment of one's life task, remaining open to opportunities for growth and development whilst realising the endless possibilities that lie within his grasp. Frankl underpins the meaning of life by reference to a suggestion by Goethe:

> How can we learn to know ourselves? Never by reflection, but by action. Try to do your duty and you will soon find out what you are. But what is your duty? The demands of each day (Frankl, 2009, p.68).

Life becomes more meaningful the more difficult it gets, if we embrace its hardships as well as its rewards. In doing so we broaden our capacity to overcome rather than endure the burdens that life may impose upon us at any given moment in time. The very fact that man's life here on earth, though unique for each individual, will inevitably end, should in itself give added meaning to life as its span is set within the realm of time. We must therefore become active and fill each day of our lives with content, "ready at all times to be called away" (Frankl, 2009, p.77).

Love, entertainment and humour, though in their minutest quantity, were "the soul's weapon for self-preservation" (Frankl, 2004, p.54). One wonders how such opportunities or emotions could arise within the confines of Auschwitz or Dachau and yet this is one man's testimony: "life is meaningful to every human being under any circumstances" (Frankl, 2004, p.65). Life takes on true meaning once man stops doubting the significance of his own existence. We have a responsibility to life for a given task that only we as unique individuals can fulfil; nobody else can complete this for us, we are irreplaceable and have only one chance to seize each opportunity along the way of fulfilling that unique task. The will to meaning involves conscious choices or decisions 'for' or towards something or someone. Once that consciousness has been awakened in an individual, he or she will spontaneously and automatically seek, find and move towards a particular goal. As cited by Frankl in *Theories of Psychotherapy,* man's decision to behave morally is not to satisfy a moral drive or to have a good conscience, but "for the sake of a cause, to which he commits himself, or for a person whom he loves, or for the sake of his God" (Patterson & Watkins, 1996, p.443). Man can surmount many obstacles, barriers and upheavals when directed and guided by the spirit; he can avail of the 'freedom to' find true meaning in life.

The stimulus for the development of logotherapy can be traced to Frankl's desire to tackle the sickness of the century. He considers that "the fight against these depersonalizing and dehumanizing tendencies, which have their roots in the psychologism of psychotherapy, has been the bright red thread that runs through the fabric of my work" (Frankl, 2000b, p.67). Frankl's theories emerged and evolved out of years of experience and observations as a medical apprentice, in particular the four years spent at Am Steinhof Mental Hospital, which led him to conclude "that which is sick is not necessarily wrong. This theory I have come to call 'logotherapy'" (Frankl, 200b, p.75). Logotherapy declares war on pathologism by promoting psychotherapy in 'spiritual' as opposed to purely 'scientific' terms. "As I have said, two times two makes four, even if a paranoid patient says it" (Frankl, 2000b, p.75). Frankl stressed the psychic health or illness of the holder of a world-view has no bearing on the correctness or incorrectness of that view (Frankl, 2009, p.33).

> Under the name of logotherapy, I have tried to introduce into psychotherapy a point of view that sees in human existence not only a will to pleasure (in the sense of the Freudian 'pleasure principle'), and a will to power (in the sense of the Adlerian 'striving for superiority') but also what I have called a will to meaning (Frankl, 1967, p.102).

Logotherapy is a development of traditional approaches of individual psychology and psychoanalysis. Traditional methods hunt around the individual's past looking for hidden complexes and symptoms upon which to address, accept and 'free oneself from' in order to 'do' or move forward. *Logos*, a Greek word, has a twofold definition of "the meaning" and "the spiritual" (Patterson & Watson, 1996, p.447). Logotherapy, as the name suggests, deals with the existential and spiritual nature of a person by delving into the core or nucleus of the personality whilst simultaneously exploring one's heights, reaching beyond that of the physical and psychic domain, to examine the spiritual dimension of man. Logotherapy suggests a freedom which originates within and from the spirit of man; it recognizes man's spirit and man's 'freedom to' make choices for himself and define who he is as an individual: "Physic the mind, and the body will need no physics" (Frankl, 2009, p.31). Unlike psychologism, which combines both aspects of man – the human spirit and the psyche – existential therapy and logotherapy consider these two aspects separately: "the fact remains that the spiritual and the psyche aspects of man must be considered apart; both represent realms essentially different" (Frankl, 2009. p.35). Logotherapy looks beyond the psyche of man and acknowledges the distress of the human spirit. Its effectiveness can only be sought by those who recognise this spiritual dimension, which can be uncovered through existential analysis, by directing the patient towards the spiritual core, leaving the ultimate decision with the client in terms of accepting or rejecting the spiritual dimension of the human psyche.

> The spirituality of man is a thing-in-itself. It cannot be explained by something not spiritual; it is irreducible. It may be conditioned by something without being caused by it. Normal bodily functions affect the unfolding of the spiritual life, but they do not cause it or produce it (Frankl, 2009, p.16).

Logotherapy aspires to educate the individual towards responsibility for one's life task. "Logotherapy sees in responsibleness the very essence of human nature" (Frankl, 2004, p.114). It strives to direct psychology towards existential analysis, which has been credited with acknowledging "man as a form of being" (Frankl, 2009, p.37). Man is therefore 'conscious' as a being and 'free' to decide who and what he is as an individual. Logotherapy aims to make man conscious of his responsibility, which arises out of his awareness of a life task or mission. Frankl suggests that logotherapy:

> seeks to bring to awareness the unconscious spiritual factors of the patient's personality, while Existential Analysis is the endeavour to enable the patient to become conscious of his responsibility (Patterson & Watkins, 1996, p.440).

Man's striving to find concrete meaning in life, that is, his will to meaning, can at times become frustrated and led Frankl to coin the term 'existential frustration'. The term 'existential' refers to existence itself, the meaning of existence or the will to meaning. Every neurosis has an existential aspect and, according to Frankl, is grounded in four different dimensions of man's being: the physical, the psychological, the societal, and the existential or spiritual dimension. Existential frustration can lead to neurosis, in which case logotherapy speaks of "noogenic neuroses" as opposed to the traditional sense of the word – psychogenic neuroses. *Noos* derives from the Greek word meaning 'mind' (Frankl, 2004, p.106). *Noetic* refers to the spiritual dimension from which noogenic neuroses emerge. Frankl emphasised that "noogenic neuroses are illness 'out of spirit' but they are not illness 'in the spirit'" (Frankl, cited in Patterson & Watkins, 1996, p.445). It is the aim of existential analytic logotherapy to help trace the source of neurotic behaviour back to its ultimate ground. The ability to transcend one's facticity is the key to overcoming existential anguish. Should the ability to tap into the transcendent unconscious become repressed, the individual may display noticeable neurotic symptoms such as "unrest of the heart" (Frankl, 2000a, p.73). Neurosis involves primarily the psychic dimension of the person; however, as suggested by Frankl:

> neurosis is no noetic, no spiritual illness, no illness of man merely in his spirituality. Much more it is always an illness of man in his unity and wholeness". Psychological complexes, conflicts, and traumatic experiences, however, are manifestations rather than causes of neurosis, which is more closely related to a developmental defect in the personality structure. Anxiety is a common factor, although it is not the cause of neurosis; however, it sustains the neurotic cycle (Frankl, cited in Patterson & Watkins, 1996, p.445).

The writer considers that existential problems, of which frustration of the will plays a major role, are therefore appropriately and adequately treated through logotherapy, "a therapy which dares to enter the specifically human dimension" (Frankl, 2004, p.107). Meaninglessness derived from a lack of awareness of a meaning worth living for has a detrimental influence on an individual. He or she gets caught in an 'existential vacuum', a place of inner emptiness resulting in despair. The existential void or vacuum which manifests as boredom is the modern-day cancer of the twenty first century. Man is faced with the burden of having to make choices; by not knowing which way to go or what to do, he or she either succumbs to conformism or totalitarianism. "Sunday neuroses" is rampant as man becomes aware of the lack of content in their personal life. The void within becomes manifest, exposing the underlying existential condition which in some cases presents as depression, aggression, addiction, suicidal thoughts and may also be endemic among pensioners, together with the aged. Lack of meaning may also masquerade as a fervourous striving to power, money, pleasure or sex.

As suggested by Frankl, humility is called for when confronted with the fact that as human beings we are by our very nature limited in our capacity to transcend ourselves and our situation; it is only when we have courage to humbly seek the originating source or spiritual dimension that we truly transcend ourselves, elevating our level of existence to that of a higher spiritual plain. Existentialists speak of transcendence in terms of 'possibility', one's 'freedom to choose' and transcend the facticity of one's situation, whereas logotherapy speaks of transcendence in terms of 'freedom to' arising out of 'spiritual freedom'. By combining logotherapy with psychotherapeutic approaches, clients can access this 'freedom to' by 'deciding for' the active pursuit of one's life task, and in doing so achieve 'freedom from' the existential anguish of the twenty-first century (Frankl, 2009).

"To be human means to be different, but also to be able to become different, that is, to change." (Frankl, 2009, p.87). Within the concentration camps Frankl experienced what it truly means to be human. Man as an individual is a unity with three aspects, the physical, the mental and the spiritual. The first two include inherited and constitutional factors, such as innate drives and together constitute the "psychophysicum" (Patterson and Watkins, 1996, p.441). Logotherapy emphasises the third dimension, the spiritual. Human existence is a combination of "man's spirituality, his freedom, and his responsibility" (Frankl, 2009, p.16). Spirituality is the first characteristic of human existence that distinguishes people from animals. Frankl firmly believed in man's spirit, as an entity in its own right, borne of the "spiritual unconscious" from which derives conscience, love and aesthetic conscience (Patterson & Watkins, 1996, p.441). By acknowledging and utilising the unlimited potential of the spiritual dimension, man has the ultimate freedom and responsibility *to* choose his essence; that is, his or her uniqueness and singularity as an individual. Once man has acknowledged his inner spirit he can achieve lasting unity, a sense of wholeness and avail of the freedom to find meaning in life.

Frankl acknowledged freedom in the face of three factors: instinct, inherited disposition and environment. Man is free to accept or reject his instincts; man's biological make-up may be a determining factor on his natural degree of personal freedom; and the environment in which man exists may also influence his freedom. However, all these factors are dependent on man's attitude and how he internalises his situation. Logotherapy teaches;

> Human freedom is in no way a freedom from conditions but rather the freedom to take a stand towards conditions. Therefore, choosing a stand towards suffering means exerting freedom. In doing so, man, in a sense, transcends the world and his predicament therein (Frankl, 1967, p.34).

Man must find resources and outlets within himself when factors beyond his control exert limitations which test his physical, emotional and spiritual capacity. Man's spirit can find meaning in the very suffering inflicted upon him, which is beyond his control, once he has accepted suffering as part of his life task, comforted in the knowledge that it is serving a greater good or is necessary to his development and maturation as a person. "In some ways suffering ceases to be suffering at the moment it finds a meaning, such as the meaning of sacrifice" (Frankl, 2004, p.117). Opportunities to find meaning in suffering lie in the way in which man bears his burden, should he find that it is his destiny to suffer. Man may not be able to alter his circumstances but he can choose to change his attitude towards his unalterable fate. To gain pleasure or avoid pain should not become man's aim, as one of the core tenets of logotherapy suggests; he should always endeavour to seek meaning in his life. He, who knows the "why" for his existence, will be able to bear almost any "how" (Frankl, 2004, p.88). This in turn leads to Frankl's third dimension of human existence, responsibility.

Individuals are responsible for their life and every human life has his or her unique task to fulfil. Life presents us with endless opportunities to fulfil and realise our life task and it is our responsibility to avail of these opportunities on an ongoing basis. But to whom are we responsible? Frankl points to conscience as the primary source of responsibility, the voice of the spirit within, urging us on to achieve our life task. It is conscience alone that serves to direct us, and has little to do with good and bad in terms of what one should or should not do. "What is good will be defined as that which fosters the meaning fulfilment of a being. And what is bad will be defined as that which hinders this meaning fulfilment" (Thorne, 1991, p.114). Those who are of a religious persuasion hear the voice of their conscience as that of God, guiding them in fulfilling their mission while here on earth. It is the view of this writer that Frankl's theory, in effect, takes into account all religious denominations and those who would describe themselves as spiritual as opposed to religious. His theory does not support or give preference to any one group; rather it encourages an awareness of the spiritual dimension of man, and is balanced and reflective in its delineation.

2.3 On the Meaning of Love

From the onset one must make a clear distinction between sexual attitude, eroticism and love. The former is centred around physical appearances, arousing the sex drive of another. Eroticism focuses upon the physic structure of another leading to feelings of infatuation, while love penetrates all layers and allows for a deeper union between two individuals on a spiritual level. "It finds its deepest meaning in his spiritual being, his inner self. Whether or not he is actually present, whether or not he is still alive at all, ceases somehow to be of importance" (Frankl, 2004, p.49). The spiritual core carries the physic and bodily characteristics towards which the sexually and erotically disposed person is attracted, "it is what 'appears' in those appearances" (Frankl, 2009, p.133). Love enables us to see and to experience the living experience of another in all their uniqueness and singularity. It involves the coming together of two individual life experiences to merge into a community of oneness leading to a monogamous relationship, marriage. It is the lover's task to be faithful and trust must be reciprocal, based on honesty. Fidelity, if demanded, will inevitably be taken as a challenge. Love is a totality, you either love or you do not really love. Within its boundaries lie enrichment; love liberates both parties yet unifies them spiritually into one. Love speaks of freedom and seeks freedom. Efforts to capture, confine or safeguard love are futile and are in direct opposition to its very essence. "I called out to the Lord from my narrow prison and He answered me in the freedom of space" (Frankl, 2004, p.97).

In the eyes of the 'other' the beloved is unique, irreplaceable and incomparable, leaving no room for the seed of jealousy to take root. If one is jealous by nature they will engender the very thing they fear. "Infatuation makes us blind; real love enables us to see" (Frankl, 2009, p.146). The essence of each individual is perceived within the union of love, their core self is visible and assessable to the other through no effort, merit or intention. Frankl regards this aspect of human interaction as 'grace'; not only is love 'grace', but also 'enchantment', enabling heightened perception of values and a wider perspective in general. Frankl also refers to a third factor that enters into love, "the miracle of love", through which a new life comes into being itself complete in its uniqueness and singularity (Frankl, 2009, p.133). Love therefore enables relationships to penetrate the physical and psychic appearances into the spiritual core of another.

Personality is more important to the lover than outward appearances. Our world extends and our perspective broadens as love allows us to experience another's personality as a world in itself. "Through the eyes of love we glimpse our spiritual soul as seen by the lover, 'love helps the beloved to become as the lover sees him'" (Frankl, 2009, p.146). Without love the true essence of the other remains hidden and inaccessible and we do not perceive the person's uniqueness.

> By his love he is enabled to see the essential traits and features in the beloved person; and even more, he sees that which is potential in him, which is not yet actualized but yet ought to be actualized...the loving person enables the beloved person to actualize these potentialities (Frankl, 2004, p.116).

Superficial love based on sexual desire and fulfilment can easily be transferred to a duplicate of the person. One is attracted to a certain 'type' as opposed to something one 'is' or 'has'. The woman or man who slavishly imitates the popular 'type' instead of creating a 'type' which expresses his or her unique qualities must therefore be unfaithful to him or herself. The body is a means of expression, expressing the character, the spiritual core, guiding one person to another through instinct. The sexual act, when expressed by the lover, is the physical expression through the body of a deeper spiritual intention. Youth, according to Frankl, must explore in order to seek out and find the right partner, one that offers comradeship, tenderness, intimacy and mutual understanding. Love is active by nature and is a direct response to life itself. Mixing and engaging with life and others can lead to love, and is key in terms of finding a cure for sexual frustration in young people. Unhappy experiences present opportunities for growth and maturation. If unresolved and unexplored unhappy experiences can lead to disappointment or resentment for those of an erotic disposition, or disbelief in the possibility or potential of inspiring love for those of a sexual disposition. Frankl contends that man ought to want to be "worthy of happiness" as opposed to wanting to be happy (Frankl, 2004, p.155).

Love is an intentional act and in its truest formation can of itself conquer death. "The existence of the beloved may be annihilated by death, but his existence cannot be touched by death" (Frankl, 2009, p.135). Love does not belong to the realm of time nor is it limited to the physical world. It belongs to the spiritual realm as its source and unity is within and through the essence of individuals, the spiritual soul of man. "The moment we experience true love, we experience it as valid for ever, like a truth which we recognize as an 'eternal truth'" (Frankl, 2009, p.143). It is the writer's contention that love is a gift and must remain a gift. We can receive love, experience love, give love but we should never seek to possess love. Frankl suggests love is available to all; however it is not utilised by all, as the laws of love surpass that of human intellect or understanding. One should never exploit love, as to know and experience real love is to glimpse an eternal truth; it is valid forever. "Set me like a seal upon thy heart, love is as strong as death" (Frankl, 2004, p.50). Love is elusive, the more you chase after love the more it will elude you. Love springs forth from within the spiritual soul of man providing an endless flow of love's energy to enrich, enhance and nourish one's life. One who actively engages with life and his fellow man with an open and contrite heart will experience love in all its richness and fullness. When the spirit remains open to life and to love it will actively flow through into one's life experiences and become embedded in the fabric of the conscious and unconscious mind. Through awareness of the existence and potentiality of love, one will begin to see the world through the eyes of love and come to realise that love exists, together with its unlimited potential, within each and every situation, experience and moment in time. This writer considers that to experience love is to encounter the source of love itself, God.

2.4 Death, Meaning and Self-Transcendence

Uniqueness and singularity are key components of human existence in terms of the meaning of human life. Man cannot avoid his human condition and must bear what Frankl called "the tragic triad of human existence; namely pain, death and guilt" (Frankl, 1967, p.25). The finiteness of man's existence 'adds to' as opposed to 'takes from' this sense of meaning. Life is a forward motion in which experiences are preserved in the past and cannot be changed, what is experienced by a person no power on earth can change.

> Not only our experiences, but all that we have done, whatever great thoughts we may have had, and all we have suffered, all is not lost, though it is past; we have brought it into being. Having been is also a kind of being, and perhaps the surest kind (Frankl, 2004, p.90).

Frankl suggests that the quality of life can never be judged by its longevity but rather by the richness of its content. Inner limits and individual differences only serve to add meaning in life and underpin one's uniqueness and singularity within the whole of human existence. If we were all perfectly formed, we could easily be replaced by another perfectly formed individual. It would appear that our very differences form the basis of our individual strength. "Without perception of the unique meaning of his singular existence a person would be numbed in difficult situations" (Frankl, 2009, p.119). Frankl (2009) uses the image of a mosaic to capture the essence of man's singularity and subsequent integration within the community when he suggests that every particle, though incomplete and imperfect in form and colour, finds ultimate meaning only from its use in the whole. "Life transcends itself not in 'length' – in the sense of reproduction of itself – but in 'height' – by fulfilling values – or in 'breadth' in the community" (Frankl, 2009, p.79). The writer concurs that such a perspective of life gives every life meaning regardless of the length of that life. By actively engaging with life and one's fellow man, man will achieve and experience wholeness or unity within him or herself and within creation as a whole. The more one forgets him or herself the more he or she will indirectly find themselves by fulfilling the simple demands of each day. By uncovering the depths of man's individuality, the spiritual dimension, one's natural response will be to reach out to life with love and in doing so achieve self-transcendence. Integration in the community should not be confused with escaping into the mass, the mob, which of itself is without consciousness or responsibility: "True community is in essence the community of responsible persons; mere mass is the sum of depersonalized entities" (Frankl, 2009, p.82).

In the face of imminent death, Frankl made a pact with heaven to preserve his mother's life by offering up his suffering. He felt 'duty-bound' to stay alive for the sake of his mother; death had meaning and living was now a task which he had to fulfil every moment of every day. The last inner freedom, the freedom to choose one's attitude in any given situation, can never be taken from a person. "It is this spiritual freedom – which cannot be taken away – that makes life meaningful and purposeful" (Frankl, 2004, p.76). We are constantly being questioned by life and our response must be "in right action and in right conduct" by taking "responsibility to find the right answer to its problems and to fulfill the tasks which it constantly sets for each individual"(Frankl, 2004, p.85).

According to Ludwig Binswanger, human existence is spiritual. The distinction of whether spirit is conscious or unconscious becomes irrelevant in the light of another distinction, whether a given phenomenon is seen as spiritual or instinctual. Drawing upon the work of Binswanger, Karl Jaspers and Martin Heidegger, Frankl arrived at the conclusion that "being human is being responsible – existentially responsible, responsible for one's own existence" (Frankl, 2000a, p.32). Existence becomes authentic when the self is deciding for itself. Unlike other therapies which focus on a two-dimensional view of existence, Frankl set about exploring the definition of existence as spiritual.

Frankl developed a sophisticated three-dimensional model from which is projected Max Scheler's concentric layer model together with the strata model (Appendix A, Fig. 1). Being human is centred around a core, which is the agent or centre of spiritual activity. The essence of man 'is' therefore spiritual and from within this spiritual dimension man can achieve unity, giving rise to the notion that "I 'am' a self" (Frankl, 2000a, p.34). Surrounding this spiritual core man 'has' a psychophysical overlay which comprises of man's physiological and psychological facticity. There exists a very sharp boundary between man's psychophysical facticity and his spiritual existence. Being human is always individualised yet integrated. When combined, the body and physic of man constitute a physophysical unit. However, this in no way represents wholeness when existence is, in essence, spiritual.

Frankl uses an analogy of the eye to highlight a very important aspect of the spiritual dimension of man. At its very place of origin, the retina of the eye has a blind spot from which the optic nerve enters the eyeball; so too the spirit is 'blind' precisely at its place of origin. The point where the spirit enters, 'original spirit', is therefore blind and unconscious of itself; the person or executor of spirit is essentially unable to reflect fully on that which he basically is, from within the depths of his spiritual core. According to the Indian Vedas, "that which does the seeing, cannot be seen; that which does the hearing cannot be heard; that which does the thinking, cannot be thought" (Frankl, 2000a, p.37). The spirit is unconscious not only at its origin but also at its height – some aspect of man keeps guard and "watches over man as if it were conscious, and yet it is at best quasiconscious" (Frankl, 2000a, p.37). Frankl concluded that the essential spiritual core of man can therefore never be fully analysed and as a result existential analysis is aimed towards an understanding of the nature of existence as opposed to an analysis of existence itself. Thus existence is always directed at something or someone other than itself, a characteristic which Frankl termed "self-transcendence", the essence of human existence. The more man forgets himself and gives of himself to another or to a cause, the more human he becomes, as man is characterised by his "search for meaning" as opposed to his "search for himself" (Frankl, 2000a, p.84).

> The eye doesn't see anything of itself. Equally, by virtue of the self-transcendent quality of the human reality, the humanness of man is most tangible when he forgets himself – and overlooks himself! (Frankl, 2000a, p.85).

As cited by Frankl, "unconscious spirituality is the origin and root of all consciousness" (Patterson & Watkins, 1996, p.441). Within the spiritual unconscious, existential analysis has uncovered religious unconsciousness. Frankl conceives of this relation in terms of a relationship between the immanent self and the transcendent

Thou. He suggests that "we are confronted with what I should like to term 'the transcendent unconscious' as part and parcel of the spiritual unconscious" (Frankl, 2000a, p.68). Whether conscious or unconscious, man has always stood in an intentional relation to transcendence. Indeed, Frankl considers, "In the solitary darkness of the 'pit' where men had abandoned me, *He was there*. When I did not know His name, He was there; God was there" (Frankl, 2000a, p.15).

In terms of 'God consciousness', man may be conscious or unconscious of the presence of God, thus forming the basis of that relationship. God is always conscious of himself. The unconscious is profoundly personal and is neither divine nor omniscient; God must not be seen as an impersonal, separate entity within man. Frankl states:

> It would be a complete misconception to assume that the unconscious is itself divine. It is only related to the divine. That man has an unconscious relation to God does not at all mean that God is 'within us' that he 'inhabits' our conscious – all this is but a notion of theological dilettantism (Frankl, 2000a, p.69).

Man's unconscious relation to God remains deeply personal and is rooted in personal decisions and existential choice, even if only on an unconscious level. Religiousness therefore stems from the personal centre and existential regions of the unconscious; it is a matter of 'choice' as opposed to an instinctual drive or inner force, merely taking place within man's unconscious. Man faces an existential choice in relation to 'God consciousness' and must therefore accept personal responsibility. "Genuine religiousness has not the character of drivenness but rather that of deciding-ness – and falls with its drivenness. In a word, religiousness is either existential or not at all" (Frankl, 2000a, p.71). Frankl suggests that the religious or transcendental aspect of the spiritual unconscious is an existential agent as opposed to an instinctual factor. Its roots are therefore of a spiritual nature rather than psychophysical. Based on this principle, unconscious religiousness is neither innate nor inherited but can be determined or influenced by cultural moulds, traditional indigenous symbols, and the examples set by our ancestors, in particular the lives of the saints and zaddiks (Frankl, 2000a).

Genuine religiousness cannot be forced or driven by an instinct, it must unfold in its own time and in its own way. Psychotherapy, if handled correctly, can, however, release unconscious religiousness in the patient. Religiousness is therefore spontaneous, an existential choice on behalf of the patient. Psychotherapy, by its very nature, is not and can never be religiously orientated. Logotherapy is therefore a supplement as opposed to a substitute for psychotherapy from which religiousness may emerge spontaneously as a by-product or side effect. Psychotherapy should never be seen as a servant to theology, to do so would diminish the service it actually performs: "one need not be a servant in order to serve" (Frankl, 2000a, p.81). The goals of religion and psychotherapy should not be seen in a similar light, regardless of the apparent overlap in terms of positive psychotherapeutic effect on the patient. The former is concerned with spiritual salvation, the latter with psychological solutions: "Religion provides man with more than psychotherapy ever could – but it also demands more of him. Any fusion of the respective goals of religion and psychotherapy must result in confusion" (Frankl, 2000a, p.80). The religious patient should be allowed to have his belief in the same way as that of the irreligious psychiatrist. It is not the job of the physician to interfere or try in any way to change the "world view" of the patient. (Frankl, 1967, p.155). In the same light the religious psychiatrist can offer comfort to the religious patient and if required assume a role similar to that of the priest. Religious goals must never be a starting point or aim of psychotherapy; they must emerge spontaneously within the therapeutic relationship between two people who choose to consider themselves religious by nature.

> Only a psychiatrist who is himself a religious person is justified in bringing religion into psychotherapy. An irreligious psychiatrist never has the right to manipulate the patient's religious feelings by employing religion as just another useful tool to try – along with such things as pills, shots and shocks. This would be to debase

religion and degrade it to a mere device for improving mental health (Frankl, 2000a, p.80).

2.5 Logotherapy in Practice

The therapist's aim is to support the patient whilst attempting to alleviate the distress of the human spirit as a result of psychic disturbance (Frankl, 2009). The therapist acts as a pilot, guiding the patient through the existential crises of growth and development. Frankl comments, "This relationship between two persons seems to be the most significant aspect of the psychotherapeutic process, a more important factor than any method or technique" (Frankl, 1967, p.137). The role of the therapist is to broaden the patient's perspective and widen their visual field. Frankl made use of logodrama, by means of improvisation, to successfully navigate the existential crisis as presented by a patient who had lost the will to live, stemming from a series of personal misfortunes. Through a visualisation technique and role play, Frankl invited the patient to view her life as if from her deathbed and from such a view point she was suddenly able to see a meaning in her life regardless of the duration of life, be it short lived or that of a person eighty years old (Frankl, 2004, p.120). Frankl also makes use of group therapy to illicit a response regarding the ultimate meaning of life in the form of a "supermeaning", suggesting another dimension beyond that of man, where the question of an ultimate meaning of human suffering would find an answer. This realm of understanding exceeds the intellectual capacities of man and requires him to "bear his incapacity to grasp its unconditional meaningfulness in rational terms. *Logos* is deeper than logic" (Frankl, 2004, p.122). As opposed to an artist who presents a final image of the world as he sees it, the logotherapist, as suggested by Frankl, acts as an eye specialist, enabling the patient to see the world as it really is: "logotherapy is neither teacher nor preacher" (Frankl, 2004, p115).

To deal with neurotic fear, which cannot be cured by philosophical understanding, Frankl devised a special technique which he called self-detachment. 'Paradoxical intention' was put forward by Frankl to deal with symptoms or situations brought about by fear, anxiety or obsessional thoughts, which are being resisted by the person. It encourages a 'flight from fear' and appears to affect a deeper level of consciousness. The logotherapist is more concerned with the patient's attitude towards his neurosis than the presenting symptoms. The technique appears rather simplistic; it encourages the very symptom most feared by the patient, which in turn brings about a reversal of attitude. Paradoxical intention breaks the cyclical effect of anticipatory anxiety, which provokes the initial symptom leading to the psychic response of anticipatory anxiety. A sense of humour is also essential for the effectiveness of paradoxical intention as it puts the patient at a distance from the anxiety itself by ridiculing his symptoms. "The neurotic who learns to laugh at himself may be on the way to self-management, perhaps to cure" (Frankl, 2004, p.127). Paradoxical intention is an intrinsically non-specific method and has proved successful in dealing with patients presenting phobic symptoms, instances of severe obsessive-compulsive character neurosis, sleep disturbance and insomnia. It is the view of this writer that Frankl strengthened the effectiveness of paradoxical intention by making references to therapists, other than himself, who achieved successful results with patients, where in some cases alternative therapies were tried, tested and failed. Patients achieved long-term benefits from the use of paradoxical intention within a short period of time.

Frankl encouraged the use of 'de-reflection' to help obsessional neurotic patients counteract compulsive inclination to self-observation, by ignoring the symptom. In support of Frankl's theory it appears logical, to the writer, for such patients to focus on their life task as opposed to the disturbing factor of the symptom itself. This in turn highlights the very dangers, as Frankl suggests, imposed by alternative approaches such as psychotherapy, which would encourage such patients to focus too much on the symptom, which in the case of the obsessional neurotic, is the disturbing factor (Frankl, 2004, 2009).

Frankl uses another approach in his model which he termed 'bibliotherapy'. He values the use of carefully selected poems and other forms of literature. The power of poetry to infiltrate the human mind must never be underestimated. As a supplement to logotherapeutic techniques, poetry can evoke a spontaneous response to the goodness and beauty of life. Frankl experienced the potent power of poetry within the depths and despair of camp life. When the harsh reality of camp life was laid bare, Frankl, whilst contemplating, unveiled the wisdom and depth of meaning contained within the lines of poetry and in doing so encountered the truth:

> I grasped the meaning of the greatest secret that human poetry and human thought and belief have to impart: The salvation of man is through love and in love...For the first time in my life I was able to understand the meaning of words, 'The angels are lost in perpetual contemplation of an infinite glory' (Frankl, 2004, p.49).

Poetry can of itself encourage the human heart and mind to venture more deeply into that private, inner world where the spirit awaits to encounter and surprise; bringing forth repressed unconscious content into conscious levels of awareness (O'Rourke, Lecture Notes TCD, 2009a). True awakenings are spontaneous and poetry has the power to arouse and evoke such reactions. Through the metaphorical language of poetry, divine energy can be approached with caution and due care to reflect the reader's level of understanding, awareness and insight. "Spirituality is about properly handling the fires, those powerful energies that flow through us" (Rolheiser, 1998, p.29). Poetry can, through the power of words and their potential for meaning, transport the reader safely to the place of originating spirit. As a result, logotherapy can avail of that unique power which is inherent in the works of carefully selected poets such as Gerard Manley Hopkins, W.B Yeats, William Blake, William Wordsworth, Emily Dickinson and Patrick Kavanagh, all of whom create a rich mosaic of spiritual awareness through varied themes and personal insights.

Summary

Victor Frankl, a Jewish psychiatrist, developed and validated a revolutionary approach to psychotherapy known as logotherapy. The essence of being human, according to Frankl, lies in the search for meaning and purpose. By taking responsibility for our existence we can respond to the questions that life asks of us. Frankl illustrates the effectiveness of his theory of logotherapy, in dramatic way in which those same theories were lived out and tested during his imprisonment in the Nazi concentration camps, in which his family, friends and fellow Jews perished. Frankl witnessed man's suffering, and observed many as they succumbed to the tragedy which engulfed them, whilst others became empowered, achieving a personal victory in the face of adversity. This study of man's survival led him to the conclusion that whilst no one is free to determine what happens, we are all free to determine our attitude to life as it unfolds, regardless of the limitations imposed upon our physical freedom. Nobody can deprive man of the power to 'choose'. Therefore, man is ultimately 'free' to decide his singularity and uniqueness as an individual. Freedom, responsibility and spirituality, the greatest of all three, merge to form the royal thread which binds man to his essence, his spiritual core. Frankl acknowledged freedom in the face of three factors; instinct, inherited disposition and environment. Man can find meaning within unavoidable suffering once he accepts it as his life's task, utilising the self-transcendent quality of the spiritual dimension. Frankl viewed love as the highest goal to which man can aspire to as it is a force which surpasses the realm of time. The aim of logotherapy, in which the relationship is central, is to encourage the client to assume responsibility for the existential or spiritual nature of their life.

Being human is centred around a spiritual core, forming the bedrock upon which man can achieve unity or wholeness. Frankl developed a three-dimensional model to explain his theory which integrates the somatic, psychic and spiritual aspects of man – a threefold wholeness which makes man complete. Man as a spiritual being has the potential for religiousness which lies within the unconscious realm. Religiousness must be spontaneous and involves an existential choice: "unconscious religiousness stems from the personal centre of the individual man rather than an impersonal pool of images shared by man" (Frankl, 2000a, p.72). Logotherapy aims to direct psychotherapy towards existential analysis, with the aim of educating the individual towards responsibility which arises out of an awareness of a life task. Logotherapy seeks freedom originating from within the spiritual dimension of the human being whilst existential therapy seeks freedom through the possibility of choice, directing man towards an inner truth which lies within the spiritual dimension of his existence. Ultimately, it is man who decides whether to accept or reject his own spirituality. Man is self-determining, deciding what his existence will be from moment to moment. The main feature of human existence is the capacity of man to rise above biological, psychological or sociological conditions, to grow beyond them. "Man is capable of changing the world for the better if possible, and of changing himself for the better if necessary" (Frankl, 2004p.133).

THREE

Spirituality: Its Essential Essence in the Work of Anthony de Mello

Introduction

Anthony de Mello, an Indian Jesuit spiritual director and retreat leader who gave workshops, conferences, and seminars all over the world, gained international popularity through his writings which incorporated stories, parables and meditations that exemplified his teachings. De Mello had a major impact on people of all faiths and beliefs in the 1980s until he suffered a fatal heart attack in 1987 in Forlorn, New York as he prepared for his annual summer lecture tour. De Mello combines spirituality with psychology in an attempt to dig deeper and awaken the heart of man to reality and to the presence of God in all things. De Mello differentiates between religion and spirituality, claiming that a healthy spirituality 'should be good to all'. "The human mind makes foolish divisions in what love sees as one" (De Mello, 1989, p.173). Spirituality, according to De Mello, involves waking up! With the discovery of the presence of God, prayer will ensue as a natural loving response to that presence. "For him the unaware life was not worth living, and his mission was to open it up" (Ford, 2009, p.103).

3.1 Anthony De Mello: His Life and Times

Anthony de Mello was born on September 4, 1931, in Bombay, to Louisa Castellino and Frank de Mello, both of whom were of Indian descent and natives of Goa. In 1947, after India's independence and the annexing of Goa, many of the natives moved to English-speaking regions and tried to maintain a Goan identity, marked by English, Indian and Goan cultural traits. De Mello and his family spoke English, and their home reflected both Western and Indian influences of the time. In 1952, the family moved to Bandra, another suburb of Bombay, where they availed of better educational facilities. From an early age De Mello was exposed to activities and services associated with the Catholic religion. The eldest of four children, Anthony was exemplary in fulfilling his Christian duties and piously indulged in teachings and practice of traditional Catholicism. His father was a kind-hearted man who cared deeply for the welfare of his family, whilst his mother had a strong personality in the sense that despite her belief and practice of the faith, she did not do so sheepishly. When Lousia died her wishes to be cremated were carried out by her family though their later request to have her buried on holy ground was refused.

De Mello attended a prestigious Jesuit school in Bandra, Bombay – St. Stanislaus High. "Spanish Jesuits were models in life for the catholic boys of their school" (Nayak, 2007, p.12). An exceptionally bright student, De Mello was gifted at languages and spoke English, Marathi and Hindi fluently. He was popular with both staff and students and was skilled in human relations. He decided from an early age, against the wishes of his parents, to become a Jesuit. Jesuits are members of the Society of Jesus, a Catholic religious order whose founder, St. Ignatius of Loyola was described by Pope Benedict XVI as "a man who gave the first place in his life to God" (Ford, 2009, pg.109). On July 1, 1947, at the age of sixteen, De Mello joined the Jesuit noviciate,

Vinayalaya, in the suburb of Bombay. "A Jesuit ripened slowly and steadily, like an apple on the tree, one among many." (Nayak, 2007, p.14). Ignatius of Loyola was a soldier prior to establishing the Society of Jesus and became the figure upon which trainees modelled their life. St. Ignatius helped people to connect their faith with their every-day lives through the compilation of the spiritual exercises, "a month long program of meditations, prayer, considerations, and contemplative practices" (Ford, 2009, p.109). Father Casasayas "taught Anthony the art of prayer and meditation" (Nayak, 2007, p.14). The young novice observed thirty days of silence, practised poverty, chastity and obedience; and learned to 'obey' like a corpse, a virtue De Mello carried out unconditionally throughout his life. Affection in the form of touch was forbidden and anything associated with emotions or feelings were stunted or cut short. Members of the Society of Jesus took on that 'Jesuit look': serious, withdrawn, somewhat artificial in feelings and emotions. Modesty, humiliation and rejection were encouraged, as was study and intellectual formation.

As cited by De Mello's brother, Bill de Mello, "Tony was born a natural priest. The Society of Jesus was home. He was the hand and the Society was his glove" [Internet]. Available at: http://users.tpg.com.au/adsligol/tony/tony2.html. [Accessed 19 March 2011]. On the 23rd March 1961 in St. Peter's, the Church of his baptism, De Mello was ordained a priest. Throughout his studies he had not shown a particular interest in theology. As a gifted student he was afforded the opportunity to study in Spain, the mother province that sent missionaries to India. De Mello became fascinated with the language associated with the Spanish mystics, Teresa of Avila and John of the Cross. Upon his return from Spain, Bill noticed that a transformation was evident in Anthony: "he seemed to have dropped the rigidity and appeared to be much more flexible in his views on church dogma and discipline" [Internet]. Available at: http://users.tpg.com.au/adsligol/tony/tony2.html. [Accessed 19 March 2011]. Father Ignacio Calveras, a great spiritual master and scholar in spiritual exercises was decisive for De Mello. His first programme had its roots in the fifteen-day Ignatian Retreat he made under Father Calveras, where he learned that the essence and purpose of spiritual exercises "were feeling (*sentire*) and tasting (*sapere*) of spiritual savour deep in the senses" (Nayak, 2007, p.17).

Though influenced by western traditions throughout his early years, Anthony exposed himself towards the later years of his studies to Indian religions such as Hindu and Jain spiritual masters, igniting his interest in the Ignatian spiritual exercises and spiritual counselling. However, De Mello had in the early years of the noviciate "already made his fundamental choice in life: to become a missionary" (Nayak, 2007, p.20). It was engraved in his heart and mind as a challenge in life. Father Edward Mann, the superior of the Jesuits in Bombay, suggested that his training as a spiritual counsellor be his niche as there was a growing need at the time to integrate psychology and psychological counselling. "People everywhere felt that a genuine spirituality was possible only when it was backed by a healthy psychology" (Nayak, 2007, p.20). In 1963 he left for America and studied for a masters degree in counselling at Loyola University in Chicago. He became familiar with various schools of psychology and mixed with free thinkers; this enlarged his cultural and intellectual horizons. He came into contact with lay people, lay thinkers, and non-churchgoers and found himself in situations that required a translation of traditional Christian and Jesuit thought into a modern world context to meet the growing needs of more secular and non-Christian individuals (Nayak, 2007, p.20). He put into practice Carl Rogers' concepts of acceptance, empathy and congruence, together with Fitz Perls's principal of 'a continuum of awareness'. De Mello applied these new psychological discoveries to the spiritual domain, forming what would later become the centre of his own approach (Ford, 2009, p.110).

In 1964 he left America to begin his formal training in spirituality in Rome. The study of spirituality in an academic context in the Roman

University appeared unrealistic and contributed little if nothing to his American experience. De Mello returned to India in 1965 and after pronouncing his final vows, which professed De Mello a permanent and fully fledged Jesuit, he worked briefly as a missionary in Shirpur, Central India. As a gifted and highly popular Jesuit his creative and dynamic approach was noted by superiors who, in 1968, appointed him as rector of Vinayalaya. De Mello focused upon personal reform as a starting point for reforming within the routine-bound Jesuit house: "his experiments were first tried in the laboratory of his personal life before applying them to others" (Nayak, 2007, p.25). He was not satisfied with a purely spiritual approach and claimed that "we should never put a spiritual patch on a psychological wound" (Ford, 2009, p.110). De Mello worked closely with Hindus and Muslims and was inspired by the life of Mahatma Gandhi, the pioneer of satyagraha, referring to him as "the great soul" (Ford, 2009, p.110). For De Mello, Christ should be emulated by Indian Christians as he had been a person that had remained true to his inner promptings. Christ was alive and fully open to the Spirit, he preached what he lived through all that he experienced, while Gandhi, who was logical and reasoned, lived what he preached. Christ was mis-interpreted by most and should, according to de Mello, be understood mythologically or poetically, as opposed to rationalistically or literally (Ford, 2009, p.111).

During the 1970s he became more and more interested in the methods and techniques of oriental spiritual masters. De Mello never quoted the scripture or teachings of different religions in support of his spiritual teachings. Such an approach was futile as there are huge variations and interpretations of such teachings. The value of a spiritual idea was to be found in relation to the impact on the life of the person who assumed it; therefore, "all that he borrowed from other religions was somehow filtered through his own personal experience" (Nayak, 2007, p.28). According to Nayak, De Mello looked for things that changed and transformed life. During this period Jiddu Krishnamirti was influential in both the East and West and inspired De Mello with his ideas on freedom in education and seeking God by abandoning the ideas we make of him (Nayak, 2007, p.28). S.N. Goenka, an Indian businessman, taught Vipassana, an ancient Buddhist meditation technique, which if practiced over a few days had the potential to bring about enormous life changes. This simplistic approach inspired De Mello and he later recommended participants of his own approach to meditation, Sadhana, to try a session of Vipassana under this master.

In 1972, De Mello settled at De Nobili College in Pune where he set up the Institute for Pastoral Counselling and Spirituality. He began his spiritual exercises and experiments in Sadhana. The Catholic Theological Society of America hailed his first publication in 1978, *Sadhana: A Way to God*, as "perhaps the best book available in English for Christians on how to pray, meditate, and contemplate" (Ford, 2009, p.114). The subtitle, *A Way to God*, throws light on the meaning of the Indian title. Sadhana brings together a variety of prayer methods to include mental, vocal and petitionary prayers with the purpose of bringing man into the presence of God and therefore into the presence of Love, Joy and Peace. With the discovery of the ensuing sense of God's presence, prayer becomes a direct response to the awareness of the Divine presence (Dych, 1999, p.8). In 1978, the Institute of Pastoral Counselling and Spirituality was renamed Sadhana Institute, which was relocated to a villa at Lonavla between Bombay and Poona, where its work was monitored. This period marked the final and most important decade in the life of De Mello, reflecting one of freedom as he opened up to the guiding Spirit in all situations of life (Nayak, 2007, p.39). Over the next nine years there followed a rich succession of books comprised of stories, spiritual exercises, story mediations, and meditations in the more formal sense. The spirituality he preached widened to universal dimensions in which all people of good will from all religions and cultures would feel at home and above all respected. "A good spirituality that is good" De Mello loved to repeat, "should be good to all" (Ford, 2009, p.124). His approach was intercultural, as he tried to cater for all religious persuasions and varying backgrounds. He focused heavily on group therapy, which included harsh and painful shock therapy, role-play, talks, and spiritual direction rather than on meditation and contemplation.

As a person, De Mello was described by his fellow Jesuits and those that knew him well as a powerful personality, a classic extrovert who loved to be the centre of attention. He embodied the notion of impermanence: "changing and accepting whatever was beautiful" (Ford, 2009, p.119). Being full of life, he was noted for his wit and humour and as quoted by a fellow Jesuit, "he was a modern mystic" and "became a spiritual master naturally" (Ford, 2009, p.119). Father Carlos Vallés, SJ, a fellow Jesuit who knew De Mello well, described him as a master of parable, of wisdom stories that made people laugh and as a gifted communicator with the ability to obtain collaborators to assist him with organising his public talks (Ford, 2009, p.122). Opinions of De Mello were of course divided; some believed he wanted to be the master in all situations and when he experimented, he did so not for himself but for all, deliberately casting himself in the light of an international Indian Guru. It was noted that he hesitated when joining in the experiments of others, an aspect of his personality which others likened to that of Mahatma Gandhi: "the lonely but in the lone centre, living and working for others" (Nayak, 2007, p.47). He fearlessly challenged people to think for themselves and had an acute skill for getting to the heart of the matter very quickly and provoke a person to think something else (Ford, 2009, p.119). De Mello was remembered by those that knew him as a seeker of the truth, "a spiritual master, a rock of faith and a beacon of light" (Nayak, 2007, p.49). As his popularity and acclaim grew to universal levels, fellow Jesuits became suspicious, envious and uneasy with his unique style which was seen by many as a mixing of oriental cocktails without the fundamental Catholic ingredients. Those who knew him least criticised him most as De Mello fearlessly wandered into different territories and utilised that which he found useful, passing it on to others. Although he moved from his traditional Catholic background, "he himself would have said it was precisely because he was so deeply rooted in the church that he discovered the freedom to find his own wings and fly" (Ford, 2009, p.119). As public opinion of De Mello remained divided he rarely focused upon it, opting instead on refocusing his attention towards his spiritual vision.

In 1986, he experienced a dark night of the soul not uncommon to followers of the spiritual path. This period of loneliness, fright and despair in which he felt abandoned by God lasted many months, yet the following year, in 1987, he appeared to be on the point of a new liberation. At a seminar a few weeks prior to his death he encouraged listeners to remind themselves each morning of death; only then would they start to live. On June 2, 1987, having arrived in North America for a six-month tour conducting various Sadhana programmes, De Mello suffered a fatal heart attack and was found "lying on the floor in a foetal position with his thumb in his mouth" (Ford, 2009, p.121). On the day prior to his death, he wrote, "I find the whole of my interest is now focused on something else, on the 'world of Spirit,' and I see everything else as trifling and so irrelevant...never before in my life have I felt so happy, so free..." (Ford, 2009, p.121). His body was flown back to Mumbai and in the church of his baptism, St Peter's in Bandra, De Mello was laid to rest. His tomb is not visible to the public as the church authorities have, for reasons unknown, exposed the Blessed Sacrament at the very entrance of the Church. His epitaph, the words of Julian of Norwich, embodied the essence of his teachings: "Sin is behovenly, but all shall be well and all shall be well and all manner of things shall be well" (Dych, 1999, p.43).

3.2 De Mello's Spirituality: Its Essential Essence

De Mello was preoccupied with the art of living spiritually, opting to experiment and share his experience with others in the hope of awakening in them a taste for spiritual growth. The framework he developed was an ever-growing spirituality as he did not structure or systematise his teachings on spirituality. De Mello was a man of religious and spiritual certitudes and his life really developed along two particular pathways, emotional and spiritual. Indeed, the Goan Catholic Church, with its rigid traditional practices, was most important in his life. An inner dawning of spiritual freedom coincided his Jesuit ordination, "taking the form of liberation from deep-rooted tension, anguish and guilt linked with an oppressive idea of God" (Nayak, 2007, p.55). By applying psychology to the problems of spiritual life, De Mello preached spirituality in a newer, fresher way, making it a joyful experience. For De Mello nothing was more practical than spirituality, as a psychologist he only had the capacity to relieve the pressure. "It's only when you're sick of your sickness that you'll get out of it. Most people go to a psychiatrist or psychologist to get relief. I repeat: to get relief. Not to get out of it" (De Mello, 1990, p.12). De Mello came to the realisation that "you can make use of suffering to end suffering" (1990, p.141). He endeavours to bring people back to what he termed the fundamentals of spiritual life, when he spoke of "mortification and fasting as a wonderful means of awakening the spirit from within" (Nayak, 2007, p.24). De Mello was of the opinion that religion and the spiritual traditions needed reform and that the Jesuit lifestyle no longer reflected the ideals of poverty and asceticism of religious life. He felt that what the Jesuits needed was the experience of stark poverty, intense prayer and the direct experience of God.

As described by Father Joseph Daoust, president of the Jesuit School of Theology at Berkeley, De Mello offered a spirituality without walls and helped people from all backgrounds "to find God in all things" (Ford, 2009, p.111). According to Daoust, it was De Mello's wholeness as opposed to his holiness that enabled him to get beneath and touch into things in a non-threatening way. De Mello had the ability to merge students' psychological struggles with his spiritual issues; "he was whole but he also made you feel the wholeness of creation and of the world's religions in yourself" (Ford, 2009, p.112). According to De Mello, the fundamental purpose of Ignatian spiritual exercises was to bring people to a state of prayer, of consolation, joyfully experiencing God's presence in all things throughout the day (Nayak, 2007, p.25). His interest in psychology led him to other religions and other spiritualities, resulting in what he called Sadhana. De Mello described Sadhana as "a way of looking at reality 'prayerfully'" (Nayak, 2007, p.36). Sadhana is a synthesis of Ignatian spirituality, of the spiritual exercises and modern psychological insights combined with Eastern spiritual methods of meditation and contemplation (Nayak, 2007, p.37).

The long-term effects of formal spiritual exercises were short-lived; Jesuits experienced a temporary change for a number of months before reverting back into their old rut. Sadhana, according to De Mello, "is very effective and will change you to the depths of your being" (Nayak, 2007, p.35). The meditations focus on silence, stillness, body sensations, thought control and breathing sensations which incorporate fantasy exercises, all of which help people "undertake a journey from the external world to the internal, creating an inner peace" that would bring the whole person to prayer, "body and soul, heart and mind, memory and imagination" (Ford, 2009, p.115). The world according to De Mello is transitory and awareness leads to the inner discovery that everything has a beginning, a moment of becoming, and an end. "Becoming fully aware of this nature of mind and being was to be the soul of spirituality" (Nayak, 2007, p.31). True happiness is the experience which stems from the freedom arising out of such a realisation. The truth one learns about oneself will ultimately set them free (Ford, 2009, p.116). Many have experienced the powerful force of Sadhana, piercing through the hardened heart to ignite the inner chambers to uncover "peace, contentment, joy, love and happiness, making prayer a delicious experience" (Nayak, 2007, p.37).

Following the publication of his work De Mello felt that spirituality could not be contained in a series of exercises. A spiritual experience is comparable only to that of love as it must be lived and experienced in order to be understood. De Mello believed that the 'shortest distance between a human being and truth is a story' (Dych, 1999, p.9). Power, for De Mello, lay not in the written word but the living word of the present, in the here and now. He found satisfaction in "stories, parables and living metaphors that contained truth but which did not bind it to words, yielding a continuous growth of meaning" (Nayak, 2007, p.57). De Mello's approach, as seen by the writer, gives the reader the freedom to decipher their own personal meaning and gain an insight into their own internal methods of perceiving reality from which old thought patterns can then be challenged and reviewed. "The words of the scholar are to be understood. As suggested in De Mello's *The song of the Bird*:

The words of the master are not to be understood. They are to be listened to as one listens to the wind in the trees and the sound of the river and the song of the bird. They will awaken something within your heart that is beyond all knowledge" (De Mello, 1982, p.4).

Words are inadequate in themselves, "they just give you a clue, a hint; they're only pointers...don't take them too literally" (De Mello, 1990, p.106). De Mello stresses the important point that words are just a signpost, they create analogies, images, but are limited. They sometimes correspond to nothing other than universal concepts which are always static, frozen labels for reality which is always in motion yet concrete. The word 'river' is static whereas in reality a river is a body of water that is constantly flowing. Every single thing in reality is unique and to avoid boredom we should avoid looking at things through our concepts. Concepts are never entirely accurate, they are merely pointers, as they miss "uniqueness, concreteness" (De Mello, 1990, p.120). Uniqueness is lost in conceptualising, all you have is an image, a label, reality must be experienced in order to discover concrete uniqueness. "You don't need to be a mystic to understand that reality is something that cannot be captured by words or concepts. To know reality you have to *know beyond knowing*" (De Mello, 1990, p.123). Words cannot give you reality, they can only consider one's perception of reality. "Reality is a whole and we cut it up to make concepts and we use words to indicate different parts" (De Mello, 1990, p.123).

Spirituality is concerned with a willingness to unlearn, to listen, "it is from the oppression of your programming that you need to be liberated. Only then will you experience that inner freedom from which all social revolution must arise" (De Mello, 1991, p.18). De Mello insists the only way to become aware of your programming is through awareness and understanding, enabling a 'break out' into reality which he describes as "lovely...it is an absolute delight" (De Mello, 1990, p.137). Agreements and disagreements have more to do with words and concepts and theories, "they don't have anything to do with truth" as "truth is never expressed in words", truth is "sighted suddenly, as a result of a certain attitude" (De Mello, 1990, p.17). The person who has reached this stage of liberty has the ability to look at life and live it with detachment, and so in freedom. "The great change that can come over a spiritual person is not that he feels he begins to change the world, but that he begins to see the world through new eyes" (Nayak, 2007, p.77).

De Mello's spirituality is marked by different stages. His idea of prayer, for example, underwent a series of transitions throughout his life. In his early years his approach to prayer reflected the teachings of the Catholic Church and the Jesuits of Mumbai, seeking union with God through mental and vocal prayers. With the dawn of his spiritual awakening, prayer meant for him the awareness with which one looks at reality outside oneself and inside oneself. In later life, prayer was for him a life led in a spirit of liberty and happiness. He did not deviate from his earlier approach to prayer but rather engaged more fully through a deeper understanding of prayer: "the heart raising to higher mystical states" through "contemplation for obtaining love, namely, seeing God in all things and at all moments in daily life" (Nayak, 2007, p.57). De Mello respected people at their own spiritual level, being at home with people of all stages of spiritual progress. Simple vocal prayer, litanies and recitations of the rosary always remained dear to him, just as the mystical heights gained through awareness.

3.3 Happiness, Pain and Suffering

His spirituality is a process of awakening to happiness and ultimately to freedom. Happiness is sought as an end to all human striving, a motivational force of all human beings. Real happiness, as suggested by De Mello, is experienced in the present, the here and now moments of life; claiming happiness is the goal of both life and spirituality. Happiness is not linked to the fulfilment of achievements or one's expectations, rather it is something to which one awakens. It cannot be acquired through one's efforts, though it is a gift available to all, at all times, in all places. It is not accepted by all as it requires opening one's eyes and seeing it. "Happiness is a state of nonillusion, of dropping the illusion...how liberating it is not to depend emotionally on anything" (De Mello, 1990, p.138). It cannot be 'experienced', it is 'uncaused', all you can do is observe opposite states of being and through observation cause them to die. De Mello describes true happiness as "unself-conscious", the moment you become conscious of your happiness you cease to be happy (de Mello, 1991, p.69). "So it is with holiness" (De Mello, 1991, p.70). It cannot be desired through the ego, but can, however, be understood through the natural and spontaneous wisdom of Nature (De Mello, 1991, p.72). The second quality of happiness is that it is effortless, and therefore it is pure grace, a gift, from which ensues a combination of peace, joy, contentment, love, compassion and thanksgiving. Like the kingdom of God, real happiness is embedded in the here and now, growing in its plenitude in the fullness of time. "Happiness and unhappiness are in the way we meet events, not in the nature of those events themselves" (De Mello, 1989, p.235).

Pain is inevitable. Not only is it a part of life's processes but is in fact necessary for life and its growth. "Every painful event contains in itself a seed of growth and liberation...an invitation and a challenge to self-understanding, self-discovery, and therefore to growth and life and freedom" (De Mello, 1991, p.157). Suffering, on the other hand, is what arises from within, it is incompatible with life, gnawing away at the spirit, killing it little by little. "There is no such thing as suffering outside; no suffering anywhere except in my individual spirit in turmoil" (Nayak, 2007, p.61). "Pain is neither positive or negative: pain is life. And life is growth and any growth has pain as one of its essential ingredients...You can comply and have no pain, and be dead: You can be free and spontaneous and have pain and be alive" (De Mello, 1995, p.11). Many revolt against pain in their life and in doing so experience pain as a chain of suffering as they do not know the art of accepting pain as an inevitable and often necessary part of life. "It can be shocking," says De Mello, "for people to discover that they themselves give expression to their suffering" (Ford, 2009, p.107). Suffering has its roots in attachment, where happiness is conditioned and based on a craving for possession or rejection of a desired or undesired object. Happiness sought in this manner is impermanent and fleeting: "The seeking becomes more important for him than finding" (Nayak, 2007, p.65). An inability to see and enjoy happiness where life takes place makes the human person restless: "The only way someone can be of help to you is to challenge your ideas. If you're ready to listen and if you're ready to be challenged, there's one thing that you can do, but *no one can help you*. What is the most important thing of all? It's called self-observation" (De Mello, 1990, p.35).

3.4 Attachment, Detachment and Discernment

The fall of attachment is the state of detachment. Awareness that the suffering lies in the person that suffers and not outside him or her is the first step towards discernment. This involves an awakening of the heart: of seeing, understanding and experiencing. Where self-observation or awareness is practiced, spirituality is not experienced as achievement but as discovery. "The Chinese sage, Lao-tse, says, 'Muddy water, let stand, becomes clear'" (De Mello, 1984, p.204). De Mello differentiates between two types of feelings, the first coming from self-glorification, which he termed a worldly feeling, the second comes from self-fulfilment, a soul feeling (De Mello, 1990, p.184). We are encouraged to return to a state of the child without being a child, when one looks into the eyes of a child one of the first qualities we see is its innocence: "it's lovely inability to lie or wear a mask or pretend to be anything other than what it is. In this the child is exactly like the rest of Nature" (De Mello, 1991, p.99). A detached person is a free person enjoying everything and every moment in life. The detached person feels intensely the pain of injustice meted out in life yet this person's attitude remains non-judgemental, there is no hate, revenge or frustration. "The detached person does not seek happiness; he experiences happiness in all situations of life" (Nayak, 2007, p.67). Spirituality is the experiencing of this joy of life, awakening to life with a continual act of thanksgiving rising from the heart. Only in a healthy body and mind can true detachment take place. Discernment is not an easy task. The attachments cling to the innermost core of the being, and detachment from them can be a long process. De Mello practiced discernment through the art of awareness by focusing all attention of the mind and body on one object: "The psychosomatic act can touch the spirit, awaken different states of consciousness and provoke deep sentiments" (Nayak, 2007, p.72). Attachment exists in the darkness of illusion, all you need to do is open your eyes and see that it is your programming, your conditioning that led you to this false belief that you really need the object of your attachment. "Even our language can be a filter. There is so much filtering going on that sometimes you won't see things that are there" (De Mello, 1990, p.133). De Mello claims that attachments are fantasies in your head, they are not a fact: "Understand your darkness and it will vanish; then you will know what light is. Understand your nightmare for what it is and it will stop; then you will wake up to reality. Understand your false beliefs and they will drop; then you will taste the happiness" (De Mello, 1991, p.9).

Through awareness the heart opens and the conscious state, thus awakened, would bring forth an experience of peace, joy, contentment, compassion, love and happiness. (Nayak, 2011, p.72). Awareness leads to the inner discovery as to the transient nature of all things, that all things are in the process of becoming, that everything has a beginning, a moment of becoming, and an end. Through an awakening and opening of the heart one is open to experience God directly. De Mello describes love as a sensitivity to reality and a wholehearted response to that reality. Attachment is a drug, a clinging that blunts your sensitivity and clouds your perception (De Mello, 1991, p.149). Therefore, true love cannot exist where you have attachment, which for the writer gives added depth and clarity to the old familiar expression "if you truly love someone set them free". Love is conscious, it entails clarity of perception and objectivity; nothing, according to De Mello, is as clear-sighted as love. Attachments destroy our capacity to love as it blocks out many things and leads to a hardening of the heart. A loving heart remains "soft and sensitive" (De Mello, 1990, p.140). If the spirit becomes unclogged and the senses open, you will at last wake up to reality and begin to perceive things as they really are, and alongside that "be entranced by the harmonies of the universe. Then you will understand what God is, for you will at last know what love is" (De Mello, 1991, p.47).

According to De Mello, one must remain cautious not to let the ego push you into awareness in an attempt to seek glorification or ego promotion. Awareness should not be your goal as to do so would make it an attachment. Change should be effortless and your 'solid attitude' and 'solid illusions' will be naturally transformed through awareness and understanding, allowing your thoughts to become fluid like water. Don't seek, limit yourself to observing. "Your attitude should be: 'I want to be aware, I want to be in touch with whatever is and let whatever happens happen; if I'm awake, fine and if I'm asleep, fine'" (De Mello, 1990, p.146). Content of awareness is less important than quality of awareness and as your silence deepens you will discover, in the words of De Mello, that "revelation is not knowledge. Revelation is power; a mysterious power that brings transformation" (De Mello, 1978, p.15). Four different stages have been noted in terms of De Mello's practice of awareness with corresponding experiences of spiritual consolation. In the first stage silence and a certain calmness is achieved through awareness of all the senses, focused on the object contemplated. During the second stage one is encouraged to contemplate the object as it is, in a non-judgemental way. The third stage consists of listening and entering into silent dialogue with the object, from which may ensue feelings of love and union with the object. In the fourth and final stage awareness brings silence: "the object being contemplated disappears and the whole mind remains objectless" (Nayak, 2007, p.74). These four steps, if practiced with an open heart over a period of time, will lead to profound discernment.

3.5 Liberty

In his later years, De Mello referred to the highest spiritual state as "liberty" as opposed to "happiness". Think of happiness as a state of inner liberty and forget the word happiness altogether. He would encourage us to substitute it with "inner liberty. Inner liberty is true happiness" (De Mello, 1995, 72). He further develops this concept in his book *Call to Love*, when he refers to inner liberty as that which enables one to marvel at creation and be forever thankful to God for the abundance of his grace which he showers on creation in the present, that is, the here and now. "The day you are happy for no reason whatsoever, the day you find yourself taking delight in everything and in nothing, you will know that you have found the land of unending joy called the kingdom" (De Mello, 1991, p.162). It is the sense of marvel like that of a small child, continuously amazed, curious and filled with a sense of wonder in all things. "This is the prerogative of the child. He is so often in a state of wonder. So he is naturally at home in the kingdom of heaven" (De Mello, 1982, p.17). It is a state in which one feels that everything in life has been a grace and a gift, nothing is taken for granted. "Freedom lies not in external circumstances; freedom resides in the heart" (De Mello, 1990, p.161).

De Mello declares 'ignorance' as the only tragedy in life, it's the source of all evil. Lack of awareness and reality is in our modern world a cancer. We need, like De Mello, to learn to understand, to wake up, to become alert and to find our own way of interpreting reality as we experience it. Awakening is simply the death of your false beliefs, your conditioning, your programming, your culture. "The end of the world for a caterpillar is a butterfly for the master. Death is resurrection" (De Mello, 1990, p.150). Until we become self-aware we have no right to interfere with anyone else or with the world. How can one "expect to see a perfect apple with an imperfect eye?" (De Mello, 1982, p.157).

De Mello was impressed and inspired by the work of A.S. Neill, well known for his revolutionary approach to education. In his book *Summerhill*, Neill states, "Freedom means doing what you like, so long as you don't interfere with the freedom of others. The result is self-discipline" (Neill, 1960, p.114). Neill asserts that "every child has a god in him. Our attempts to mold the child will turn the god into a devil" (De Mello, 1990, 179). It was through experience that Neill discovered that when the child feels loved, he or she will be okay and will start to treat others as he or she has been treated. Give others the freedom that is theirs, support them with love and you will see miracles. Love propels us into positive action, whereas inner conflict will project violence, fear and even war. When we fail to address our inner conflict we will soon discover that we cannot quench fire with fire. The root of all evil, as De Mello aptly puts it, lies in ignorance, and therefore is "within you" (De Mello, 1990, p.183).

Self-change involves insight, understanding that all you need in life you already possess, all you have to do is to see it. As Leo Tolstoy so eloquently captures in the dying word's of his character Ivan Ilyich, when on his death bed he looks into the eyes of his wife whom he deeply despised though his life and in despair ponders the question "What if I really have been wrong in the way I've lived my whole life, my conscious life?" (Tolstoy, 2006, p.98). The awakened person, according to De Mello, no longer dances to the tune of society but rather to the music that derives from the interior of their soul. He or she no longer experiences unbearable loneliness but will find that they are truly content and at peace in their aloneness. Awaken your senses and be amazed by your ability to enjoy intensely the simple pleasures of life and you will no longer pursue the artificial stimulants. De Mello suggests we stop looking for things, there isn't anything to look for, all we have to do is simply look. "Excuse me,' said the ocean fish…'can you tell me where to find this thing they call the ocean?' 'The ocean,' said the older fish, 'is the thing you are in now.' 'Oh, this? But this is water. What I'm seeking is the ocean,' said the disappointed fish as he swam away to search elsewhere" (De Mello, 1982, p.12).

Knowledge and information are not enough, to know something is not the same as being aware and feeling it. De Mello speaks of coming to your senses and nourishing your soul by getting in touch with nature – "sunsets", "a good movie", "a good book", "enjoyable work" and "good company" – in an attempt to break the cycle of addiction to artificial pleasures in life (De Mello, 1990, p.184). St. John of the Cross shared also in the belief that "when the spirit and senses are pleased, every part of a man is moved by that pleasure and delight of the senses" describing the spirit as the "highest part" and the sensual nature as the "lowest part" of man (St. John, 2003, p.11). St. John gives further explanation of this notion based on the Gospel teaching: "That which is born of the flesh is flesh, and that which is born of the Spirit is spirit" by pointing out that pleasure born of the senses is fulfilled and ends with sensuality, and that love which is born of the Spirit is fulfilled by the Spirit and can only find rest and a sense of wholeness within the Spirit of God, which causes love to grow (St. John, 2003, p.13). De Mello advises that one should wake up, be alert and live a soulful life, then you will see transformation and you will soon discover what it means to be in the world but not of the world. "Be silent and contemplate the dance. Just look: a star, a flower, a fading leaf, a bird, a stone…any fragment of the dance will do. Look. Listen. Smell. Touch. Taste. And, hopefully, it won't be long before you see him – the dancer himself!" (De Mello, 1982, p.14).

3.6 A Spirituality within the Christian Existentialist Tradition

De Mello's spirituality is imbued with clear intercultural and inter-religious traits. His interest was to experiment and discern that which was good and true in all spiritualities and traditions. His writings reflect a growth in this multi-spiritual dimension, offering a wholesome wisdom that has something positive and good to offer all men: "He was someone who was able to transcend lines" (Ford, 2009, p.113). Such an inter-religious synthesis might appear to some as a sort of spiritual amalgam, leading to accusations of syncretism, while others classify him as a New Age writer. De Mello remains firmly rooted in his Christian Catholic conviction and with the help of all beings, all cultures and religions tries to understand and experience it in its depth. "His sole aim in digging deep into Eastern spirituality was to show that it could admirably complement Christian and Western approaches to life" (Nayak, 2007, p.90). There lies, doubtlessly, an effort to point out the spiritual richness of humanity when experiences are made accessible to all instead of trying to contain them with fixed barriers of a community or religious orientation. A good spirituality does not separate people but seeks to unite all, bringing good health to all, not just Catholics, as Christ preached and reminded us: "there are many rooms in my Father's house". "The religion that makes people good makes people bad, but the religion known as freedom makes all people good" (De Mello, 1990, p.183). De Mello was in search of the living God and through other people he encountered God. Father Daoust was of the opinion that De Mello "felt many people's views of institutional religion were projected onto God and, as a result, created fear and anxiety in them" (Ford, 2009, p.113). The church in which De Mello preaches is the one in which the faithful worship: "the Father in spirit and truth" (John 4:23).

From the onset De Mello wanted to make clear and for people to understand "that religion is not – I repeat: not – necessarily connected with spirituality" (De Mello, 1990, p.21). His audience was essentially made up of religious people, who had a normal theological and spiritual formation but some of whom were suffering from an overdose of ill-served Christian spirituality in religious communities. His deeper intention was to shake them out of their routine approach to spirituality and to bring them to the source of life. Those that came to him for help found that they were exposed to more psychology than prayer and spirituality. "The important religious distinction is not between those who worship and those who do not worship but between those who love and those who don't" (De Mello, 1988, p.61). These sentiments of De Mello resonate deeply with the writer as she shares the view that God is love. The writer concurs with De Mello's suggestion that love is an outward motion; by giving love, we receive love. Through love we become whole, fulfilled, healed and no longer perceive differences as a barrier but come to appreciate and accept the unique quality of all things in relation to the whole of creation. Through love we will come to understand that love is indeed the bedrock upon which the whole of creation is united into one. Love, for this writer, is the most powerful force which is freely available to all of mankind, as the seed of love lies within each soul from the moment of its conception, binding it eternally to its divine creator, the God of Love. When reality is perceived through the eyes of love we come to an awareness of the interconnectedness of all things, the unity that exists within creation leading the writer to conclude that though we are individual and unique we are united as one in love.

For De Mello the living Christ is not a mere verbal proclamation, and through psychology people encounter themselves and the natural flow of life within them: "it is the expression of faith, that is, what bursts forth from the roots of one's being" (Nayak, 2007, p.79). It is probably better to bear witness to Jesus Christ in the silent living testimony of life than in shallow wordy proclamations. Imitating the eternal behaviour of Christ will not bring about self-change, it's a question of becoming like Christ through understanding, insight and awareness: to think like Jesus, to love like Jesus, to live in truth like Jesus (De Mello, 1990). We need to be awake and aware of reality moment by moment. "Ever since God created the world, his invisible qualities, both his eternal power and his divine nature, have been clearly seen; they are perceived in the things that God has made. So those people have no excuse at all!...instead of worshipping the immortal God, they worship images made to look like mortal human beings or birds or animals or reptiles" (Roman 1:20-23). The presence of God within and throughout creation highlights the immanence of God, the transcendent aspect of God, who chooses to surround, permeate and reside within our very being to encompass all things seen and unseen.

Jesus Christ occupies the central place in his thought; however, he did not make explicit verbal references to Christ in his teachings or writings in Christological terms. "What was needed was not so much a discourse about Jesus Christ but a spiritual outlook in life that was certainly Christ-centred" (Nayak, 2007, p.78). Through the generations, Christianity has been reduced to a set of labels through the over-development of theologising and conceptualising, particularly in Europe. As a result the mystical experience has diminished and a catechism of knowledge is in place which no longer seeks to kindle the fire for discovering and experiencing God (Nayak, 2007, p.80). "The fact is that you are surrounded by God and you don't see God, because you 'know' about God. The final barrier to the vision of God is your God concept. You miss God because you think you know. That's the terrible thing about religion. That's what the gospels were saying, that religious people 'knew' so they got rid of Jesus. The highest knowledge of God is to know God as unknowable...The one who knows, does not say; the one who says, does not know" (De Mello, 1990, p.102). According to De Mello, to really know Christ is to be transformed by what one knows (De Mello, 1982, p.112). The writer recalls a question once posed by a spiritual healer during a talk he was giving in Dublin in 2006: "If we were all rounded up and brought to court for being Christians, would there be enough evidence to convict us?" People have become desensitised to the plight of their neighbour, which begs the question 'who is my neighbour?' Jesus came for all men, therefore, all men are my neighbour, including those of another religious orientation. If, as De Mello quite accurately points out, we cannot love the brother we can see, how can we ever love the God we cannot see?

De Mello's attitude and approach to prayer mirrored that of Brother Lawrence's spiritual insights into the heart of God, "He is within us; we don't need to seek Him elsewhere" (Lawrence, 1982, p.54). As with De Mello, Scripture revealed to him his body's spirituality: "it says my body is God's temple, the spirit's dwelling place". Whilst pondering on the meaning of these lines, De Mello enters into dialogue with God about the body and listens as God speaks to him (De Mello, 1984, p.24). Brother Laurence in his writings reveals that the heart is a chapel into which we can go anytime to talk to God and believes it is a serious mistake to think of prayer time as being different from any other time: "the most perfect union with God is the actual presence of God. Although this relationship with God is actually spiritual, it is quiet dynamic because the soul is not asleep, but powerfully excited" (Lawrence, 1982, p.65). The Indian poet Rabindranath Tagore once wrote, "God wants his temple built of love, but men bring stones" [internet, p.6]. Available at: http://users.tpg.com.au/adsligol/tony/tony2.html. [Accessed 19 March 2011]. De Mello was willing to open his heart and discover for himself God's message, seeking depth and personal understanding in his attempt to communicate with the Divine:

> The spiritual man searches all things, even the deep things of God. For by this general and simple wisdom is understood that which the Holy Spirit says through the Wise Man, namely: That it reaches wheresoever it wills

by reason of its purity; that is to say it is not restricted to any particular object of the intellect or affection (St. John, 2003, p.59).

God speaks to the soul by a single act of contemplation which can never be fully comprehended by the human intellect or understanding. The writer resonates with the sentiments of St. John that through an awakening of the senses, God draws us to him and once strengthened and nurtured he draws "forth the soul from the life of sense into that of the spirit" in which faith, hope and love will be required to sustain life in the Spirit (St. John, 2003, p.25). De Mello's writings appear to be in line with the teachings of St. John: "You must learn to move out of the area of feeling, sensing, loving, intuiting. That is the area where contemplation is born and prayer becomes a transforming power and a source of never-ending delight and peace" (De Mello, 1978, p.17). God is now leading us to another road, a road based on contemplation as opposed to meditation, sustained through trust in God. It is not the way of reason, imagination, or meditation but the way of blind faith through perseverance in prayer. It requires no effort other than to be aware, attentive and alert to the presence of God in the here and now, moment by moment. Kahlil Gibran, in his book *The Prophet,* questions so aptly "what is prayer but the expression of yourself into the living ether?" (Gibran, 1926, p.89). In his introduction to Sadhana, De Mello makes reference to a Hindu guru who taught him that the art of prayer was simply a matter of breathing in and out: "The air you breathe is God. You are breathing God in and out. Become aware of that, and stay with that awareness" (De Mello, 1978, p.7).

Summary

The research has shown that De Mello was indeed fearless in his search for the truth. His great devotion to the Catholic faith became the bedrock which afforded him the mystical freedom to journey in faith into unfamiliar territory, seeking out what was good and true in spiritual practices from Eastern culture in an attempt to complement Christian and Western approaches. In doing so, De Mello's intercultural approach sought to understand, experience and highlight the spiritual richness of humanity. Religion, according to De Mello, is geographical, influenced and conditioned by the culture from which it emerges, whereas spirituality, as shown by the research, is universal, it embraces all people to include Christian, non-Christian and doubters alike. The spirit is present not only in that which is spiritual but in all things that are human "nothing human is foreign to the Spirit" (Dych, 1999, p. 26). The research provides a clear delineation of De Mello's approach to spirituality, inciting man to wake up, be alert and allow God to act. Man is encouraged to embark upon a journey towards awareness, becoming ever more attuned to the present where the presence of the Spirit is visible and at work in all of creation, enabling a 'break out' into reality. Man's spontaneous reaction to the immanent presence of God leads to a life lived in prayer, awakening the heart of man and allowing the transforming power of God reshape and remould that individual as He wills. Before one embarks upon such an inner journey, one must realise that God is beyond words, concepts, or doctrinal formulas. God is the known unknown and life is forever a mystery to the human mind. All that is needed is trust and faith in God, captured so eloquently in De Mello's chosen epitaph: all shall be well, and all shall be well, and all manner of things shall be well!

CONCLUSION

This study has been carried out with a view to exploring the theme of spirituality and counselling within an existential framework and asks the question 'Does the counsellor possess the skills and insights to hold this sacred space?' The research presents a comprehensive overview of existentialism and existential therapy in which a number of significant philosophers of varying religious and non-religious orientations are considered. These include Jean-Paul Sartre, Irvin Yalom, Victor Frankl and Anthony de Mello. The aim of this research then is to place emphasis on the spiritual dimension of man and to highlight the sacred space occupied by the modern-day counsellor. The writer holds the view that counsellors have a duty of care to explore spiritual and existential issues with the patient and must endeavour to explore in depth their own spirituality in order to fully understand the true nature of man.

The existential approach to therapy appears to reflect and move in synchronicity with life's natural flow, rendering it a highly valid and effective response to the existential anguish which has engulfed the mindset of the twenty-first century. It endeavours to explore a number of key existential themes such as death, freedom, isolation and meaning. With the emphasis on the relationship and the need to adapt therapy and one's approach to meet the needs of the client, it is the writer's view that within this elusive framework lies a new dawning, through an awareness of the spiritual dimension of man. Based on the author's research in this study, it would appear that the advent of existentialism, though present for centuries, surged following World War as humanity sought to overcome the horrors of Nazi Germany, to find meaning in life. It did not endeavour to justify what had taken place, but sought to rise above the pain and suffering, enabling man to experience once again the endless possibilities so abundant in life. Existentialism spoke of freedom, the freedom to choose one's path, to emerge from the ashes and transcend the facticity of one's situation.

The research provides initially a precise delineation of Sartre's anti-religious approach to existentialism. For Sartre our existence is nothing more than a brute fact, the 'world' is our creation, we are superfluous; we are a mere product of nature without intrinsic value and hope. It is the writer's contention that Sartre, a renowned philosopher of the twentieth century, though he clearly understands what it means to exist, fails to understand the true nature of man. His philosophy lacks the unifying power of originating spirit, be it God or that of a higher power or source. His reductionist view of man is sub-human in that it reduces man to a two-dimensional being. The spiritual soul of man remains dormant in Sartre's philosophical ruminations, leading the author to conclude that as a result, the individual remains fragmented and ultimately contributes to his or her existential anguish. Sartre appears to have maintained a pragmatic approach to life, remaining, as it were, 'faithful to the earth'. He was only concerned with the practical demands of living; Sartre either consciously or unconsciously chose not to explore the hidden gem within the core of his 'Being', the spiritual dimension of man through which we become whole and unified in the Spirit of oneness. How can man truly live if he only seeks to exist? How can man be truly free if he has not learned to conquer death itself? Sartre, much to his credit, did consider the one ultimate freedom that could never be taken from the individual, that being the freedom to 'choose'. Failing to choose is also a personal choice. Sartre highlights the role of responsibility and free choice in determining the direction of one's life. Choice rests at the core of his philosophy.

Chapter Two, however, turns to Christian existentialism and provides a comprehensive overview of Victor Frankl, the author's philosopher of choice through which to ground this body of research. Frankl was a central figure in the development of existential therapy. As can be seen from the research, Frankl's insights and reflections into the human condition project man as a three-dimensional being comprised of somatic, mental and spiritual dimensions. It is the integration of this threefold wholeness that makes man complete. Without the spiritual dimension, according to Frankl, man cannot achieve this wholeness. Each individual life has a unique concrete meaning to fulfill, regardless of the personal or external circumstances. Frankl links freedom of choice with responsibility. It is up to each individual to decide 'from what' he is driven and 'to whom' he is responsible. Frankl sums up these two facets of the human condition through a simple admonition from Maria von Ebner-Eschenback: "Be the master of your will and the servant of your conscience!" (Frankl, 2000a, p.59). To his enormous credit he rehabilitated the conscience and defined 'good' as that which fosters fulfilment of meaning and 'bad' as that which hinders fulfilment of meaning fulfilment. Frankl suggests that morality no longer defines that which is good and bad and sees the conscience as the means to discover meaning (Thorne, 1991, p.114). Conscience acts as a prompter, indicating the direction we should go in a given situation.

Through his observations and personal experiences in the Nazi death camps, Frankl came to the realisation that whilst one could not control or determine what happened to them, they could at least control their response to the fate that had befallen them. These men, women and children emerged from the camps as true survivors; though they had lost everything, they had managed to preserve a vestige of spiritual freedom and independence of mind. Frankl gained a valuable insight into the nature of man, "that everything could be taken from a person but one thing: the last of the human freedoms – to choose one's attitude in any given set of circumstances, to choose one's own way" (Frankl, 2004, p.75). Though subjected to degradation and inhuman violence on a daily basis, the people who availed of this spiritual freedom appeared mentally and physically healthier. An air or calm permeated these persons' existence in the midst of the insanity which unfolded around them. Frankl concluded that a spiritual centredness was the foundation which rendered them powerful rather than powerless in the face of adversity.

It is this enduring spiritual freedom, available to all, which ultimately gives life its very meaning and purpose. The author suggests that such a perspective, though it may not change personal circumstance or the problems we face, does however increase our ability and effectiveness in dealing with the problems that life throws our way. Whilst we cannot predict, plan for, or control many aspects of future experiences, we can decide here and now that whatever the circumstances we may find ourselves in, we can and will respond as persons of inner strength and resilience. We can choose our attitude and through spiritual centredness find strength and peace within the eye of the storm. When Frankl bore witness to man's inner strength and to the fact that the last of the inner freedoms cannot be lost, the words of Dostoyevsky resonated deeply with him: "There is only one thing that I dread: not to be worthy of my sufferings" (Frankl, 2004, p.75). It is ironic, yet a great comfort to believe, that man could in fact discover the greatest liberation of all, in the midst of pain, suffering and captivity.

Frankl's life journey gives testimony to the potentialities that lie within the grasp of each and every man; the decision and responsibility is ultimately one of personal choice, with life offering a constant flow of opportunities to allow us actualise our true potential. Frankl believed that within every desperate situation there is always a shred of meaning to be found. "That is why every man is even ready to suffer, on the condition, to be sure, that his suffering had a meaning" (Frankl, 2004, p.117). Frankl's witness to meaning led to the development of his theory of logotherapy, which put forward the notion that life becomes more meaningful the more difficult it gets.

Logotherapy is an analytic process which takes into account instinctual facts alongside existential realities. It examines and seeks to uncover the true meaning of man's existence by actively looking towards the future. The search for the deeper meanings in life is a universal theme and is as relevant today as it was over seventy years ago, as people still try to make sense of life or some aspect of living. The very act of questioning makes us human. Meaninglessness, derived from a lack of awareness of a meaning worth living for, can lead to feelings of despair as one is encumbered by an 'existential vacuum', which is the mass neurosis of our present time. The void becomes manifest, exposing the underlying existential condition and often presents as depression, aggression, addiction or suicidal thoughts. Logotherapy can help in that it aspires to educate the individual towards independent responsibility. Each man must become conscious of his or her responsibility to find a deeper, concrete meaning in life. Human existence is always directed towards something, someone, other than itself and it is this very characteristic of human nature which Frankl termed 'self-transcendence'. The self-transcendent quality of human nature is most tangible when man overlooks and forgets himself. Existentialists speak of transcendence in terms of 'possibility', one's freedom to choose and transcend the facticity of one's situation. Logotherapy speaks of transcendence in terms of 'freedom to' arising out of spiritual freedom. By directing psychotherapy towards existential analysis, the starting point of which is 'consciousness of responsibility', and supplementing it with logotherapy, clients can access this 'freedom to' by 'deciding for' the active pursuit of one's life task. In doing so, clients can achieve 'freedom from' the existential anguish of the twenty-first century. Logotherapy therefore stems from the spiritual, whereas existential analysis is directed towards the spiritual. Frankl asserts that sickness in the somatic or mental layer does not emanate from within the spiritual dimension. While one may experience illness of the mind or body, the human spirit, or noetic core, remains healthy. Logotherapy uncovers the fluid and spontaneous nature of our spiritual existence. Our human existence is elevated to new spiritual heights once lived in and through the Spirit from which it originated.

In Chapter Three the writer turns to another major Christian existentialist in the work of Anthony de Mello, a Jesuit priest who was remembered by those who knew him well as a seeker of the truth, a spiritual master, a rock of faith and a beacon of light. De Mello successfully sought out and combined what was good and true in spiritual practices from Eastern culture in an attempt to complement Christian and Western approaches. The spirituality he preached widened to universal dimensions in which people of good will from all religions and cultures were included and above all respected. His intercultural approach had a major impact, helping people from all backgrounds, to find God in all things. De Mello differentiated between religion and spirituality, claiming a healthy spirituality should be good to all and he challenged people to think for themselves. Suffering, according to De Mello, is inevitable and necessary for growth, life and freedom, as within each painful event there lies the seed of growth and liberation. He came to the realisation that you can make use of suffering to end suffering. For De Mello nothing was more practical than spirituality; however, he was not satisfied with a purely spiritual approach to personal growth, claiming, "we should never put a spiritual patch on a psychological wound" (Ford, 2009, p.110). He tried to show in wise and humorous ways that the psychological walls that imprison people were simply mental constructs with no basis in reality. For De Mello the unaware life was not worth living, and he made it his mission to awaken people to an awareness of God's presence in their lives, as Christ himself had done. The author concurs with De Mello in his assertion that Christ had been a person who had been true to his inner promptings. Christ was very much alive because his teachings came from the experience of life, he preached what he lived. Getting to know one's inner Spirit involves interior conversations. Before embarking on this inner journey, De Mello stresses that God is beyond words, concepts, or doctrinal formulas. The highest knowledge of God is to know God as the 'great unknown'. To really know God is to be transformed by what one knows. Religion, as De Mello envisaged, is geographical, influenced and conditioned by the culture from which it emerges. Spirituality, as shown by the research, is universal. It embraces all peoples to include Christian, non-Christian and doubters alike. All that is required by man is trust and faith in God. De Mello believed in the transient nature of all things, that everything has a beginning, a moment of becoming, and an end. To become aware of the transient nature of life was for De Mello the soul of spirituality. De Mello describes love as a sensitivity to reality and a wholehearted response to that reality; nothing is as clear-sighted as love. Love propels man into positive action, whereas inner conflict will project violence, fear and even war. Enlightenment, as cited by De Mello, involves seeing people as they are, not as we wish them to be, leading the writer to conclude that in seeing them we must also accept them in their totality just as they are.

Lack of awareness and reality in our modern world is a cancer. The writer agrees with De Mello's assertion that until man becomes self-aware, he or she has no right to interfere with anyone else or with the world. As suggested by De Mello, how can one expect to see a perfect apple with an imperfect eye. In light of De Mello's findings the writer concludes that within a counselling profession, self-awareness is paramount in order to stimulate growth and awareness of the client's awakening spirituality. The author values the existential emphasis on freedom and responsibility and the person's capacity to redesign his or her life by choosing with awareness. She advocates the practice of self-awareness put forward by De Mello through which one uncovers spirituality; however, the author suggests that greater emphasis needs to be directed to one specific attitude, self-acceptance. Whilst self-awareness uncovers the spiritual dimension of man, the writer considers self-acceptance as the narrow door through which one enters the spiritual realm. To acknowledge one's spiritual core is not the same as entering in and choosing a spiritual centredness as the foundation for one's existence. How can man gain mastery over the art of living in the external world if he or she has not yet accepted the Spirit of one's life internally? Man is questioned by life in a bid to rouse man from the slumbers of his existence into the fullness of life as a spiritual being. An encounter with the core self, in the writer's opinion, is in fact a direct encounter with God or the originating Spirit. By choosing to integrate that spiritual presence into one's life, man must confirm that choice on an ongoing basis, as Frankl suggests, in right action and in right conduct. Self-acceptance is, in this writer's opinion true acceptance of God, leading ultimately to acceptance of the Spirit of one's life. It is only then that man will experience a fundamental change, not in the sense of changing 'who' he is but in changing 'what' he is. In the light of the research findings, this writer concedes that once open to the transcendent, man's existence will undergo a transition from a sub-human to a spiritual existence, allowing the individual 'become' what he or she has always been, a spiritual soul. To reject any part of the human self is to reject in part the originating Spirit, rendering man unable to access in full the true potential that lies therein. The rejected, tarnished or fragmented parts of the individual must first be brought into consciousness. Through self-awareness and self-acceptance, these facets of the individual become instrumental in bringing the person to their core encounter with God. To become aware of one's human imperfections and to fully accept 'all' that one 'is' is a humbling experience, leaving man's spiritual core open to the transforming power of Spirit, therefore enabling transcendence. De Mello suggests:

> The spiritual quest is a journey without distance. You travel from where you are right now to where you have always been. From ignorance to recognition, for all you do is see for the first time what you have always been looking at. Who ever heard of a path that brings you to yourself or a method that makes you what you have always been? Spirituality, after all, is only a matter of becoming what you really are (De Mello, 1991, p.178)

When conditions are created within the therapeutic relationship for such spirituality to emerge, the therapeutic value of the process is enhanced as a result. Within the therapeutic relationship much will hinge on the therapist's capacity to be present with his or her client. The spiritual thread in Carl Rogers' client-centred approach emerged through his understanding of subjective phenomena and of interpersonal relationships, leading him in the end to embrace what he described as "the transcendent, the indescribable, the spiritual" (Thorne, 1992, p.22). Rogers' deep respect for the person and trust in the actualising tendency enabled many to discover "that at the deepest centre of the person and infusing the organismic self is the human spirit which is open to the transcendent" (Thorne, 1992, p.105). The writer does not claim to offer transforming insights but seeks to shine light on aspects of counselling which she considers beneficial to the therapeutic process, enabling access to the fullness of being. She considers self-acceptance, in light of one's imperfections, a significant step in terms of accepting and engaging fully with the Spirit of one's life. It is from the depths of our 'Being' that we uncover the living potential to reach new and unimagined heights. Rogers spoke of "inner spirit touching inner spirit" and of a therapeutic relationship transcending itself and "becoming part of something larger" (Rogers, Thorne, 1992, p.106). The effect is totally transforming for it enables transcendence to occur so that a new perspective can be achieved. Rogers concluded:

> The only real reality I can possibly know is the world as I perceive and experience it at this moment. The only reality you can possibly know is the world as you perceive and experience it at this moment. And the only certainty is that those perceived realities are different (Rogers, cited in Thorne, 1992, p.106).

The effective counsellor can only lead or point man towards his or her spiritual core, leaving the ultimate decision with the individual whether or not to accept or reject their spiritual dimension. The writer suggests it is the presence of Spirit within the spiritual encounter which heals, transforms and integrates man into wholeness.

Based on the research the author concedes that existential analysis, supplemented with logotherapy, provides a sound philosophical base on which to build a personal and unique therapeutic style because it addresses itself to the core struggle of the contemporary person. Creating a meaningful life is about finding the right attitude and becoming absorbed in that process. Logotherapy breaks through self-imposed barriers, liberating the client's true potential which is bound up in the spiritual dimension of his or her being. "The logotherapist's role consists of widening and broadening the visual field of the patient so that the whole spectrum of potential meaning becomes conscious and visible to him" (Frankl, 2004, p.115). From such a perspective the individual can venture forth into the fullness of life, to uncover his or her unique life meaning. By taking responsibility and actively choosing to accept the Spirit of one's life on an ongoing basis man can lead a soulful existence. The research has shown how we discover our potential inwardly, yet true meaning is found in the world around us and is very much an outward motion which connects us to our external environment and fellow man. The more we forget ourselves the more we find our true meaning and indirectly discover who we are as individuals. As the research indicates, we must look to conscience as a guide to prompt us along our spiritual path. Through the Spirit we are gently called to have faith in an inner knowing that our life is serving a purpose far greater than our intellect can fully comprehend. So have faith, have hope and above all allow the energy of the Spirit, which is love itself, propel us into positive action.

BIBLIOGRAPHY

American Bible Society (2005) *Catholic Good News Bible.* China: The Bible Societies/Collins.

Brys, A. and Pulickal, J. (1995) *We heard the Bird Sing.* India: Gujarat Sahitya Prakash.

Cochrane, A.C. (1956) *The Existentialists and God: Being and the Being of God in the Thought of Soren Kierkegaard, Karl Jaspers, Martin Heidegger, Jean-Paul Sartre, Paul Tillich, Etienne Gilson [And] Karl Barth.* Philadelphia: Westminster Press.

Cohen-Solal, A. (2005) *Jean-Paul Sartre – A Life.* New York: The New Press.

Corey, G. (2001) *Theory and Practice of Counselling and Psychotherapy, Sixth Edition.* USA: Library of Congress.

De Mello, A. (1978) *Sadhana: A Way To God.* New York: Image Books.

De Mello, A. (1982) *The Song of the Bird.* New York: Doubleday.

De Mello, A (1984) *Well Springs: A Book of Spiritual Exercises.* New York : Doubleday.

De Mello, A. (1987) *On Minute Wisdom, 4th Edition.* India: Gujarat Sahitya Prakash.

De Mello, A (1988) *Taking Flight: A Book of Story Meditations.* New York: Doubleday.

De Mello, A. (1989a) *Prayer of the Frog Vol 2.* India: Gujarat Sahitya Prakash.

De Mello, A (1989b) The Heart of the Enlightened. New York : Doubleday.

De Mello, A. (1990) Awareness: The Perils and Opportunities of Reality. New York: Doubleday.

De Mello, A. (1991) *The Way to Love.* New York: Doubleday.

De Mello, A (1995) *We heard the Bird Sing.* India: Gujarat Sahitya Prakash.

Dych, S.J.W. (1999) *Anthony de Mello.* New York: Orbis Books.

Edmund, C. and McGinn, B. (1996) *Everything as Divine: The Wisdom of Master Eckhart.* USA: Paulist Press.

Flynn, T.R. (1997) *Sartre, Foucault and Historical Reason - Volume 1.* University of Chicago: Chicago Press.

Flynn, T.R. (2006) *Existentialism: A Very Short Introduction.* USA: Oxford University Press.

Ford, M. (2009) *Spiritual Masters For All Seasons.* New Jersey: Hiddenspring.

Frankl, V.E. (1967) Psychotherapy and Existentialism – Selected Papers on Logotherapy. U.S.A.: Penguin Books.

Frankl, V.E. (2000a) Man's Search for Ultimate Meaning. New York: Basic Books

Frankl, V.E. (2000b) *Recollections – An Autobiography.* USA: Basic Books.

Frankl, V.E. (2004) *Man's Search For Meaning.* UK: Rider.

Frankl, V.E. (2009) *The Doctor and the Soul.* Germany: Souvenir Press Ltd.

Gibran, K. (1926) *The Prophet.* London: Pan Books

Guerlac, S. (1997) *Literary Polemics: Bataille, Sartre, Valery, Breton.* Stanford, CA: Stanford University Press.

Heidegger, M (1962) Being and Time. UK: Blackwell Publishing.

Hergenhahn, B.R. and Olson, M.H. (2007) *An Introduction to Theories of Personality Seventh Edition.* New Jersey: Pearson Education Inc.

Jacobs, A. (2002) *Poetry for the Spirit.* London: Watkins Publishing.

John, St. (2003) *St. John of the Cross: Dark Night of the Soul.* NY: Dover Publications, Inc.

Kaufmann, W. (1956) *Existentialism from Dostoevsky to Sartre.* USA: Princeton University Press.

Kierkegaard, S. (1940) *Stages on Life's Way.* NJ: Princeton University Press.

Lawrence, B. (1982) *The Practice and the Presence of God.* USA: Whitaker House.

Macann, C. (1993) *Four Phenomenological Philosophers: Husserl, Heidegger, Sartre, Merleau-Ponty.* London: Routledge.

Methuen (1948) *Jean Paul Sartre - Existentialism and Humanism.* UK: Methuen & Co. Ltd.

Monte, F.C. and Sollod, N. (2003) *Beneath the Mask: An Introduction to Theories of Personality: Seventh Edition.* USA: Hamilton Printing Company.

Nayak, A. (2007) *Anthony de Mello: His life and his Spirituality.* Ireland: Columba Press.

Neill, A.S (1960) *Summerhill: A Radical Approach to Child Rearing.* New York: Hart Publishing.

Patterson, C.H. and Watkins, C.E. (1996) *Theories of Psychotherapy.* USA: HarperCollins.

Rolheiser, R. (1998) *Seeking Spirituality.* Great Britain: Clays Ltd.

Rolheiser, R. (2005) *Forgotten Among the Lilies.* USA: Doubleday.

May, R., Angel, E. and Ellenberger, H.F. (1958) *Existence: A New Dimension in Psychiatry and Psychology.* New York: Basic Books.

Solomon, R.C. (1974) *Existentialism.* New York: Random House.

Thorne, B. (1991) *Person-Centred Counselling – Therapeutic and Spiritual Dimensions.* UK: Whurr Publishers Ltd.

Thorne, B. (1992) *Carl Rogers.* London: Sage Publications Ltd.

Tillich, P. (2000) *The Courage to Be.* USA: Yale University.

Tolstoy, L. (2006) *The Death of Ivan Ilyich.* UK: Clays Ltd.

Van Deurzen, E (2002) *Existential Counselling and Psychotherapy in Practice: Second Edition.* London: Sage Publications Ltd.

Woolfe, R., Strawbridge B., Dryden D. and Dryden W. (2010) *Handbook of Counselling Psychology: Third Edition.* London: Sage Publications Ltd.

Yalom, I.D. (1980) *Existential Psychotherapy.* New York: Basic Books.

Yalom, I.D. (1989) *Love's Executioner and Other Tales of Psychotherapy.* Library of Congress Cataloging-in-Publication Data: New York.

Yalom, I.D. (1998a) *The Gift of Therapy: An Open Letter to a New Generation of Therapists and Their Patients.* New York: Harper Collins Publishers.

Yalom, I.D. (1998b) *The Yalom Reader: Selections from the Work of a Master Therapist and Storyteller.* New York: Basic Books.

Yalom, I.D. (1999) *Momma and the Meaning of Life: Tales of Psychotherapy.* London: Piatkus.

Yalom, I.D. (2005) *The Schopenhauer Cure.* Library of Congress Cataloging-in-Publication Data: New York.

Yalom, I.D. and Leszec, M. (2005) The Theory and Practice of Group Psychotherapy: Fifth Edition. USA: Basic Books.

Journals

Yalom, I.D. (2002) Religion and Psychiatry. *American Journal of Psychotherapy*, Vol 56, no. 3, pp. 301.

Encyclopedia Articles

Encyclopedia Article (2009)*Existentialism. The Columbia Encyclopedia, Sixth Edition.* New York: Columbia University Press.

Online Sources

Beginnings of Logotherapy, p.1 [internet]. Available at:
http://www.logotherapyinstitute.org/creation.html
[Accessed 22 November 2010].
Tony deMello – a biography, [internet]. Available at:
http://users.tpg.com.au/adsligol/tony/tony2.html
[Accessed 19 March 2011]

Unpublished Material

O'Rourke, M. (2009a) Existentialism, Existential Psychotherapy and Logotherapy, TCD, Lecture Notes November 2009.

O'Rourke, M. (2009b) Yalom's Answer to the Crucial Questions of Meaning, TCD, Lecture Notes November 2009.

O'Rourke, M. (2010) Spirituality and Counselling: Do we Have the Knowledge and Skills To Hold this Sacred Space, TCD, Lecture Notes November 2010.

Notes, TCD (2009) Existentialism/Humanism (3rd Force), Session 8.

APPENDIX A

Victor Frankl's three-dimensional model of human reality.

The peripheral psychophysical layers encompass a spiritual personal centre. Only the spiritual core warrants and constitutes oneness and wholeness in man. Wholeness refers to integration of the somatic, psychic and spiritual aspects. It is this threefold wholeness that makes man complete.

Frankl replaces the vertical hierarchy of unconscious, preconscious, and conscious strata with the model of concentric layers, a model propounded by Max Scheler.

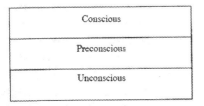
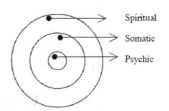

Frankl combined the strata model with the layer model and made them into a three-dimensional structure. Now the two former models have been reconciled, as it were, having become the two-dimensional projections of a three-dimensional model that more accurately depicts the human reality we are describing (Frankl, 2000a, p.34)

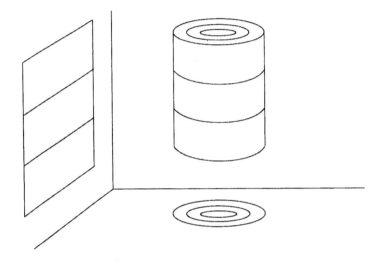

Fig. 1: Frankl's conceptualisation of the nature of man

The following variation on the **prayer by Saint Francis** (A Christian prayer which dates back to 1912) was delivered by Mother Theresa when she addressed the United Nations in 1985:

Make us worthy Lord to serve our fellow men throughout the world,
who live and die in poverty and hunger.
Give them through our hands, this day, their daily bread
and by our understanding love give peace and joy.
Lord, make me a channel of thy peace.
That where there is hatred I may bring love,
That where there is wrong, I may bring the spirit of forgiveness,
That where there is discord, I may bring harmony,
That where there is error I may bring truth,
That where there is doubt I may bring faith,
That where there is despair I may bring hope,
That where there are shadows I may bring light,
That where there is sadness I may bring joy.
Lord, grant that I may seek rather to comfort than to be comforted,
To understand than to be understood,
To love than to be loved.
For it is by forgetting self that one finds.
It is by forgiving that one is forgiven,
it is by dying that one awakens to eternal life.
Amen.

Printed in the United States
By Bookmasters